PURPLE COW
TO THE RESCUE

PURPLE COW
TO THE RESCUE

by

Ann Cole, Carolyn Haas, Betty Weinberger

Illustrated by True Kelley

Little, Brown and Company   Boston / Toronto

Also by Ann Cole, Carolyn Haas, and Betty Weinberger

I Saw a Purple Cow: And 100 Other Recipes for Learning
(with Faith Bushnell)

A Pumpkin in a Pear Tree: Creative Ideas for Twelve Months of Holiday Fun (with Elizabeth Heller)

Children Are Children Are Children: An Activity Approach to Exploring Brazil, France, Iran, Japan, Nigeria and the U.S.S.R.
(with Elizabeth Heller)

By Carolyn Haas, Ann Cole, and Barbara Naftzger

Backyard Vacation: Outdoor Fun in Your Own Neighborhood

ILLUSTRATIONS COPYRIGHT © 1982 BY TRUE KELLEY

COPYRIGHT © 1982 BY ANN COLE, CAROLYN HAAS, BETTY WEINBERGER

FIRST EDITION

Library of Congress Cataloging in Publication Data

Cole, Ann.
    Purple Cow to the rescue.

    Summary: Suggests a wide range of activities which help you learn about yourself, become more independent, prepare for school, enjoy traveling and moving, and rest after or during a busy day.
    1. Creative activities and seat work — Handbooks, manuals, etc. [1. Amusements] I. Haas, Carolyn. II. Weinberger, Betty. III. Title.
LB1537.C568   649′.51   81–17156
ISBN 0–316–15104–1   AACR2
ISBN 0–316–15106–8 (pbk.)

The authors are grateful for permission to reprint the following poems:
"Five Years Old" from *A Pocketful of Poems* by Marie Louise Allen. Text copyright © 1957 by Marie Allen Howarth. Reprinted by permission of Harper & Row, Publishers, Inc.
"The Birthday Child" from *Round the Mulberry Bush* by Rose Fyleman. Copyright 1928 by Dodd, Mead & Co., Inc. © renewed 1955 by Rose Fyleman. Reprinted by permission of the publisher.
"Bedtime" from *Eleanor Farjeon's Poems for Children*. Originally published in *Over the Garden Wall* by Eleanor Farjeon, copyright 1933, © 1961 by Eleanor Farjeon. Reprinted by permission of J. B. Lippincott, Publishers.
"Bending Places" by Nancy Mack from *Wake Up Beautiful World* by Upstarts, Inc. Copyright © 1974 by Upstarts, Inc. Reprinted by permission of Sue Blum on behalf of Upstarts, Inc.

HAL

Published simultaneously in Canada
by Little, Brown & Company (Canada) Limited

PRINTED IN THE UNITED STATES OF AMERICA

The Purple Cow is indebted to Marilyn Marlow for finding it a happy home at Little, Brown.

The Purple Cow is also grateful to the authors' brothers and sisters, for it was the family times they shared during their childhoods that inspired many of the ideas in this book. The authors dedicate *Purple Cow to the Rescue* to Ellen Slavin (Ann), Sandra Barz, Jim and Stewart Buhai (Carolyn), and Jean Kent (Betty), with love.

Introduction

The Purple Cow is back again! This time she comes to the rescue with hundreds of new and imaginative activities to help you through almost any situation: cleanup time or moving day, the last stretch of a car or bus trip, a *different* birthday party every year. Who hasn't wished for creative ideas at times like these?

The activities have been grouped into six key areas that every home or school will find useful: *Getting to Know and Like Yourself* (ways to build a positive self-image); *Learning to Be Independent* (doing things for and by yourself); *Learning the Basics* (skill-building by working with scissors, crayons, paint, and clay); *Traveling* (enjoying the hours on a plane, train, bus, or car); *Moving* (tips for a smooth departure or a warm welcome); and *Winding Down* (quiet breaks in a busy day).

However, there's no need to confine yourself to the boundaries of any one chapter when you're looking for help. By quickly skimming through the entire table of contents, you'll find many ideas to adapt "to the moment." A family game in the "Travel" section or a chalk project from the "Basics" might be just what you need when you're winding down or planning a newcomer's party. With a little ingenuity, a Pop-up Puppet could become a birthday favor, or a Marble Raceway, a "map" of your new neighborhood. The possibilities for creativity can stretch as far as your imagination.

The six chapters respond to some of the changing needs of today's families: more working mothers and "weekend fathers," who need to make their limited time with their children really count; growing numbers of single parents, making it necessary for children to take on added responsibility and to become independent at an earlier age; frequent adjustments to new people and unfamiliar places, since one out of five families relocates each year. This book presents some helpful solutions to new problems.

Purple Cow to the Rescue, like its well-loved predecessor, *I Saw a Purple Cow,* encourages learning by doing. By following the step-by-step "recipe" format and using easily collected household "ingredients," like yesterday's newspaper, even the busiest parent or teacher can get a child involved in a game or a project in no time. While the original Purple Cow book provided a preschool "curriculum" for the younger set, this sequel focuses on a broader age range. Toddlers and older brothers and sisters are all included, too, since variations just for them often appear under the heading "Another Way."

Purple Cow to the Rescue offers both one-to-one and group activities, emphasizing special sharing times at home with the family or in the classroom. Group projects (arts and crafts, indoor and outdoor games, puppetry, and cooking) are ideal for libraries, Sunday schools, day-care centers, recreation programs, scout troops, or just a small group of neighborhood kids who get together to play. Grandparents, teachers' aides, nurses, and baby sitters — anyone who works with young children — will welcome the many useful ideas for simple individualized activities.

A new feature, designed to help a teacher or parent zero in on the needs of a particular child or group, is the *Learning Chart* that accompanies each chapter. The charts are divided into columns, each denoting an area of learning: Movement and Motor Coordination, Reading and Math Skill-Building, Language Development and Communication, Imaginative Play and Self-Expression, Problem-Solving and Discovery, and Creativity and Making Things. To find the activities that best develop the specific learning goal you have chosen, simply run your finger down the appropriate column, stopping wherever you find an "X."

As you can see, *Purple Cow to the Rescue* is a "multiple choice" book to use in a way that's best for you. The underlying theme of every activity is to help a child feel confident and successful. Children feel good about themselves when they can do things independently, from zipping zippers to setting the table to concocting an Anything Soup. *Purple Cow* comes to your rescue with fresh ideas and an easy approach to the challenges and fun of growing up.

Ann Cole, Carolyn Haas, Betty Weinberger

Contents

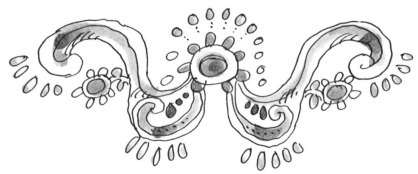

PURPLE COW TO THE RESCUE . . . When You're Getting to Know and Like Yourself

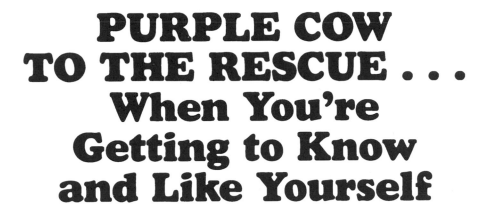

It's

- liking your face in the mirror
- learning about your body and how it moves
- accepting changes as you approach each new stage
- being proud of your name and the many ways that you're different from others
- feeling special on *your* birthday.
- And most of all, it's feeling good about growing up being you!

By playing Body Talk, or a game that signals your feelings, with a friend, you'll become aware of other people's feelings as you're learning more about yourself.

TAKE A LOOK AT YOURSELF

Everyone is different. Everyone is special. Take a look in the mirror and you'll see some of the special things that make *you* different from everyone else.

Here's a poem you can say while looking at yourself in a full-length mirror. Once you have tried these two verses, substitute other words about yourself. I like my SMILE; my TEETH; my EYES; my NOSE; and so on. And don't leave out the most important verse, "I like MYSELF, I'm special . . ."

I'm One of a Kind

I'm one of a kind.
I'm special,
I'm special, don't you see?
I like my FACE,
It's special —
My face could only be . . . me.

I'm one of a kind.
I'm special,
I'm special, don't you see?
I like my NAME,
It's special —
My name could only be . . . me.

Now look in the mirror up close. Can you observe your face carefully enough to draw a picture of it? Find some crayons and try. Take another good look in the mirror and compare yourself with your drawing. Did you put your ears in the right place? You know the color of your eyes, but did you notice how far apart they are? Are your eyebrows thick or thin? Just for fun, try making faces at yourself in the mirror. Can you draw all of your different expressions?

Next time you look at your face, will you notice new things about yourself that make you one of a kind?

Me-Doll

Do you know where your body bends? Can you count how many joints or bending places you have? To show you where all the different parts of your body are connected, make a jointed Me-Doll, just like you.

YOU NEED: cardboard
scissors
brad paper fasteners
crayons or felt-tip markers
yarn
glue

YOU DO:

1. Cut cardboard into shapes that look like the parts of your body and attach them at the joints with the brad fasteners.

2. Use crayons or markers to make your face and glue on yarn to make hair.

3. Now bend your puppet to do what *you* can do.

15

Bending Places

Words and Music by Nancy Mack

Chorus:

A   E⁷   A   E⁷   A   ⅞.

Bend-ing pla-ces, bend-ing pla-ces, bend-ing all a-bout.

A   E⁷   A   E⁷   A   E⁷   A

Do you know your bend-ing pla-ces? Come and let's find out. My

A   E⁷   A   E⁷   ⅞.

1. arm bends at the shoul---der and at the el-bow, too. My
2. leg bends at the hip   and al---so at the knee. My
3. head bends at the neck.   That's where it turns a-round. I

E⁷   ⅞.   ⅞.   A

wrist is where my hand bends, and see what my fin-gers do! My
foot bends at   the an---kle, and my toes bend too, you see? My
bend my whole self at the waist, that's how I touch the ground!

Bend each part of your body as you sing about it, and then during the chorus let yourself go and bend everything! Sing the song again and let your Me-Doll bend with you.

You can even bend your body to make *letters* and *numbers.* Which letters need a friend to help?

BODY TALK

Did you know that you can *talk* with your body? Without speaking at all, you can use your face, eyes, and the way you move to tell another person what you are thinking, how you feel, and what you like to do.

Try having a "conversation" with a partner, using only body language to describe your favorite activities.

Tell without Talking: A Guessing Game

1. Act out something *you like to do,* for example, jumping rope, riding a bike, making pudding, or blowing bubble gum.
2. Have your partner guess what you are doing while you shake your head "yes" or "no," the simplest body language of all!
3. Now switch roles — it's your turn to guess!

4. Next, use your body to act out what you are *imagining,* while the others guess what you have in mind. Without saying a word, pretend you are

   - just waking up
   - frosting a cake
   - trying to balance on a two wheeler
   - stepping over a mud puddle

(continued on next page)

17

What else can your imagination tell your body to do?

5. Now imagine you are an object or an animal — something you could *never* really be — and act it out. Bounce like a giant beachball or a tiny Ping-Pong ball; or just be a bubble . . . POP! Can you float like a feather blowing in the wind, pop like popcorn popping, or puff up like a muffin growing bigger in the oven? How would you spin like a spider or jump around like a frisky puppy?

Shadow Talk

When you're outdoors in the sunlight, you have a buddy to move about with — your shadow. Can you pat your shadow on the head or touch its toes? What happens when you hug your shadow? Wave good-bye to your shadow and watch it run away.

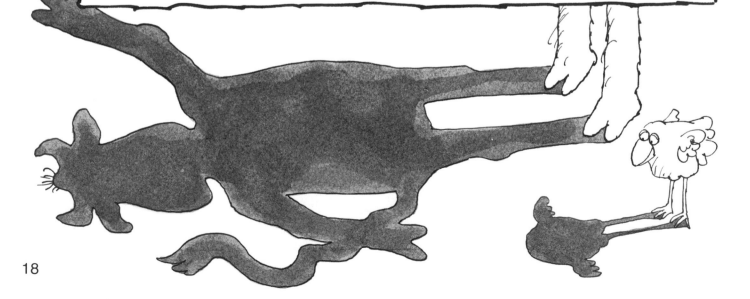

Pass the Message

Can you imagine sending *messages* to your friends without writing or saying a word?

1. For this game, everyone sits in a circle, holding hands.
2. The player who has been chosen as the starter squeezes the hand of the person next to him, who then passes the "squeeze" along so that it moves all around the circle from hand to hand.
3. Everyone tries to sit still and keep a straight face so no one will know where the squeeze is.
4. When the squeeze finally returns to the starter, he smiles and nods his head "yes," to show that the right message made it home.
5. The player on his right then sends the next squeeze on its trip around the circle.

Think of other ways to relay your messages. Use your fingers to form a letter, number, or shape in the next person's hand, or to send along a tickle or a rub. You could also give a *face* message by turning to the next person and passing along a smile or frown, a wink or a nod, or even a nose wiggle! Of course, you could always whisper a message that will make someone in the group feel good.

S.O.S.: Send Out Signals

Your body can send out all kinds of silent signals or messages to *tell how you feel.* Even animals let you know how they feel by the way they move their bodies. Have you ever noticed how a cat arches his back when he's scared? How does a dog show you that she's happy?

To play S.O.S., use your whole body to act out how you're feeling. Then as others sense your mood, they can respond to your signals by coming to your rescue.

1. Ask a grown-up to help you think up some typical situations that bring out different kinds of feelings:

You feel *scared* that a bee might sting you.
You feel *proud* because you just learned to do something new all by yourself.

2. Take turns acting them out. While one person is pantomiming his feelings, everyone else must watch carefully to get his message.
3. Some clues for the audience to look for are the changing expressions of the eyes and mouth, exaggerated gestures of the hands and arms, and the ways the actors hold their bodies when they are sitting, standing, or walking. Every movement, by any part of the body, is a signal that tells you how a person feels.
4. As soon as someone catches on to what the actor is feeling, that person *joins* him on stage and responds to his S.O.S. He might comfort him if he's sad, or take his hand if he's scared.
5. As others understand the actor's signals, they too can join in, and before long, everyone will "get into the act."

Changing Faces

Now that you are more aware of the signals people send, you'll know how to look at faces in a new way. Even while watching TV or looking through magazines and newspapers, you'll find that faces signal feelings.

YOU NEED:

shoe box with lid
scissors
magazines and newspapers
3 cardboard tubes (paper towel tubes work best)
glue
crayons

YOU DO:

1. Cut a large oval out of the box lid for a face.
2. Make three pairs of holes on opposite sides of the box, just large enough for the tubes to fit through.
3. Next cut out pictures of faces from magazines and newspapers, noticing the feelings that they show: happy, sad, tired, scared, angry, surprised, and so forth.
4. Cut each face into three parts: eyes, nose, and mouth, and sort all the parts into piles.
5. Paste two or three *sets* of eyes around the middle of one of the cardboard tubes, noses on the next, and mouths on the third. Be sure to center all the cutouts. (You could also draw on the features.)
6. Then push the tubes through the holes in the box, with the eyes on top, noses in the middle, and mouths on the bottom.
7. Now replace the lid on the box, twist the tubes, and watch the faces change. Roll a smile, a frown, some sleepy eyes or teary ones.
8. Another twist! Have some fun mixing up the expressions too. Can you make a face that laughs while it's crying?

21

VOICES

There are many ways that people know who you are. Besides knowing how you look and move, they know you by your voice. Pick up the telephone and call someone you talk to often.

How do you think he could tell it was you? Is your voice high or low? Loud or soft? Do you talk fast or slowly? Do you say "you" or "y'all"?

Even when you were a tiny baby, your family always knew your own special cry, just as they know your voice today.

YOUR NAME

You were given your name on your *birthday,* and it belongs only to you. Do you know how your family chose *your* name? Some children are named after a grandparent, like Timothy Buckingham Chattlesworth II, or for a famous person that their parents admired. Many names came from the Bible: Adam, Ruth, Matthew, Deborah.

Years ago many people took their name from the work that they did — Baker, Goldsmith, Cook, and Shoemaker — and sons often took their father's first name for their last name — Robertson, MacDonald, or O'Brien.

Lots of people have *nicknames.* Do you? Nicknames usually come from special things about you: your looks, your size, the way you talk. Have you heard of Wilt the Stilt? Fat Albert? Nicknames are often shortcuts, like Clem for Clementine or Chris for Christopher. Sometimes, they show your place in the family, like Junior or Sis.

Some nicknames are just plain silly, like "Boo" or "Goopers." Ask your parents if there is a funny story to go with *your* nickname.

Name Nonsense

Make up a silly sentence about yourself using the first letter of your name.

Examples:

My name is **S**teven and I look like **S**piderman!

My name is **C**arolyn and I walk like a **C**rocodile!

My name is **S**arah and I like to eat **S**napdragons!

Make up more silly sentences using the first letter of your name over and over again.

Betsy **b**lows **b**roken **b**ubbles.
Danny **d**oesn't **d**ig **d**andelions **d**uring **d**inner.
Harry **h**ates **h**eavenly **h**iccups.

If you **s**ay your **s**illy **s**entences **s**wiftly, **t**hey'll **t**urn into **t**ongue **t**wisters!

What's My Name? (A Guessing Game)

1. One player thinks of a person everyone knows well, like a teacher, the mailman, Charlie Brown, Curious George, and so forth.
2. He gives a few clues to help the other players uncover the name.

I can be found in a _____ (book, comic strip, on television).
My name begins with _____ (S for Santa Claus).
I like to eat _____ (spinach, like Popeye; honey, like Pooh Bear).
What's my name?

3. The others take turns guessing, and the first player to say the right name gets to be the next mystery person.

A parent or older child could think up some names to get the game started.

Nameplates

You'll feel proud to see your name in print. Here are *four different ways* to make a sign for your desk at home or school, or a license plate for your bicycle.

1. Look through newspapers and magazines to find all the letters in your name. Cut them out and paste them on heavy cardboard or a paper plate. Decorate with picture cut-outs that tell about you.
2. Write your name on a strip of cardboard, then glue yarn or macaroni over the letters. You can also form the letters with pipe cleaners or cut them out of sandpaper. Now feel the letters with your fingertips. Can you close your eyes and spell out your name?
3. What's the *shape* of your name? Find out by drawing an outline around it. Can you turn your "name shape" into a picture?
4. Try "animating" your name. Add arms and legs to the letters to set them in motion.

Put your animated name on peel-off labels or masking tape to mark your lunch box, baseball mitt, and books so they won't get lost. What are some other things you need to label?

Bookplates

To make bookplates, just print or write your name on index cards. Decorate them with crayons, felt-tip markers, or stickers, or hunt through magazines, newspapers, or comics to find pictures that you like. Paste a bookplate inside the cover of your favorite books. Then if you lend or lose a book, it can find its way back to you.

my favorite socks!

THE SPECIAL YOU

It's not just your name, your face, your voice, and how you feel about things that make you special. What you like to play, wear, eat, and do also make you "one-of-a-kind." Make a book about what you like best with a place for *you* on every page.

Put Yourself in the Picture

YOU NEED:

cardboard or construction paper
crayons or felt-tip markers
a Popsicle stick or tongue blade
glue
yarn
large paper plates (with no design)
cloth or paper scraps
scissors
tape
a notebook ring (optional)

YOU DO:

1. Make a "me-puppet" by drawing a picture of *your face* on a cardboard or paper circle and gluing it to the top part of the Popsicle stick. To make your puppet look even more like you, use a snapshot of your face.
2. Next, glue on some yarn the same color as your hair.
3. Use paper plates for the pages. On each page, draw a picture of yourself doing something *you* like to do: petting a dog, reading a book, or eating an ice-cream cone. (Use the cardboard circle as a guide for the head so your drawings will be the right size.)
4. Color or paste on clothes you'd wear when doing that activity. Now cut a line at the neck so you can slide your "me-puppet" into the picture. (You can tape a little pocket on the back of the paper plate to keep the puppet in place.)

cut slit

tape pocket on back of plate

26

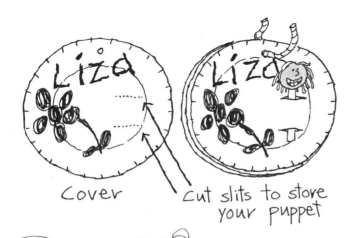

Cover

Cut slits to store your puppet

5. For a cover, write your name across the top of a paper plate and decorate it. Cut two slits (see illustration) to store your puppet.
6. Punch a hole in each plate near the top and push a notebook ring through, or use yarn to hold your round book together.
7. Now as you flip the pages, put yourself into *each* picture and tell a story about what you're doing!

BIRTHDAYS

People are always changing—no one stays exactly the same. When you look at old family snapshots or home movies, are you surprised how much *you've* changed?

An easy way to *see* change is to watch yourself grow, by marking your height on a floor-length mirror every few months or measuring the inches to be let down on last year's skirt or jeans. Every time you need a haircut, you can see that part of you is growing quickly.

Adding new pages to your "round book" (see Put Yourself in the Picture, p. 26) is another way to mark your progress, because what you like changes too. BIRTHDAYS help you to count these changes, year by year.

Please, everybody, look at me!
Today I'm five years old, you see!
And after this, I won't be four,
Not ever, ever, any more!
I won't be three — or two — or one.
For that was when I'd first begun.
Now I'll be five a while, and then
I'll soon be something else again!
by Mary Louise Allen

Add-a-Year Candle

A birthday candle, too, can help you mark off the years.

YOU NEED:

a small cardboard box or Styrofoam block for
  a base
a cardboard towel tube for the candle
scissors
construction paper
masking tape
glue
crayons or felt-tip markers

YOU DO:

1. Turn the box upside down and cut a circle in the bottom, the same width as the tube.
2. Cover the box and tube with construction paper.
3. Next push the "candle" through the hole and tape it securely underneath.
4. Glue on a red flame made of paper or cellophane.
5. Now decorate the base with crayons, markers, or stickers, including your name and birth date.
6. Each year, write your new age on a colorful band of paper and glue it onto the "candle."

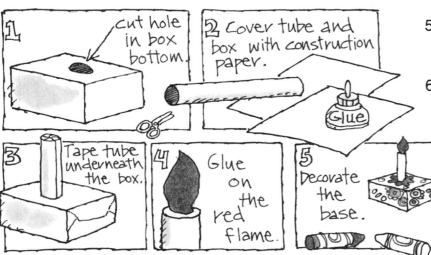

Then every time you celebrate your birthday, you can watch the stripes grow on the "candle" as you grow up too!

We all feel special on our birthdays and wish the rest of the world would notice, too. Let everyone know today's *your* day by wearing something special: a crazy hat, a new hairstyle, brightly colored socks or hair ribbons, maybe some new shoes or a special shirt.

Birthday Shirt

YOU NEED:

iron-on patches or tape (plain or print)
scissors
an oversized T-shirt
iron
laundry markers

YOU DO:

1. Using iron-on patches or tape, cut out the letters of your name, a large number showing your age, or a birthday design, like a cake with candles.
2. Have someone help you iron the pieces onto the T-shirt, following the directions on the package.
3. You could also use a laundry marker to draw a picture or write a personal message. (Be careful, the ink isn't washable.)
4. Surprise your friends and family by wearing your special shirt on *their* birthdays too!

Will it still fit you next year?

Birthday Buttons

Look for a slogan button around your house and use it as a base for your very own birthday button. Draw a circle on cardboard by tracing around a jar lid, the bigger the better! Then cut it out and glue it to the button. Make up a slogan to let everyone know that today is your birthday; for example, "It's My 'B' Day" or "Hug Me — I'm Seven."

On cardboard, trace around a jar lid and cut it out.

glue the cardboard to the button.

Another way to feel good on your birthday is to give a greeting card or a present to *someone else* — a friend who's sick in bed, a favorite teacher, or maybe even a grandma or grandpa in your neighborhood whose *own* grandchildren live far away.

I'M 7 TODAY!

29

Party Treats

Everyone loves having a birthday party! Here are some delicious ideas for treats to serve, whether you're celebrating with your friends at home or with your class at school.

CAKE CONES

Instead of the usual cupcakes, surprise your friends with some that look just like ice-cream cones!

YOU NEED:

cake mix
flat-bottomed ice-cream cones
white frosting mix
food coloring (several colors)
flavorings: peppermint, lemon, orange, etc.
toppings: sugar sprinkles, gumdrops, M&Ms,
  carob chips, cinnamon red hots, etc.
candles (optional)

YOU DO:

1. To make the batter, follow the directions on the box of your favorite cake mix.
2. Pour the batter into flat-bottomed ice-cream cones and place them on a cookie sheet or muffin tin.
3. Have an adult help you put them into a preheated oven, and bake according to the time instructions given for cupcakes.
4. Mix the frosting, following the steps on the package.
5. For different-colored and -flavored icings, divide the mixture into several small bowls, adding a few drops of food coloring and flavorings to each batch.
6. Now frost the cake cones and decorate with sprinkles and candies.

For a final touch, put a candle in the center of each one.

Another way: Create cupcake surprises. Using a yellow or white cake mix, make the *batter* different colors instead of the frosting, just as you did in step five. Then frost the cake cones with the *same* icing so they'll all look alike. You won't know what color you chose until you take a bite!

DO-IT-YOURSELF CAKE TRIM

Another new twist to the usual birthday cake is a Do-It-Yourself Cake Trim.

1. Make or buy a plain sheet cake and several frosting tubes; then have all your guests join in the decorating.
2. On slips of paper, write down some trimming ideas, and ask each person to pick one out of a box or bag.
3. Turn off the lights and lead everyone in singing "Happy Birthday to You." Carry in the cake with the candles burning brightly!
4. Have the birthday child make a wish and blow out the candles.

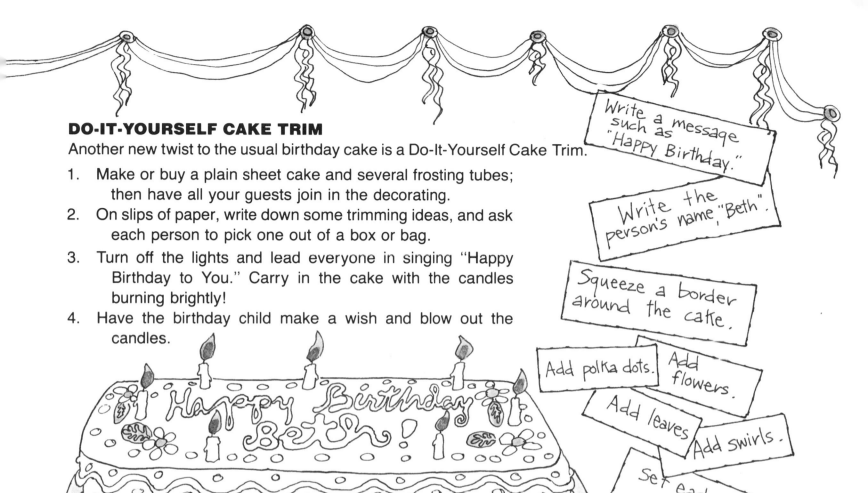

Write a message such as "Happy Birthday."

Write the person's name, "Beth".

Squeeze a border around the cake.

Add polka dots.

Add flowers.

Add leaves.

Add swirls.

Set each candle in place.

Party Food Favors

Popcorn balls and pretzels can be prepared in advance or made and enjoyed right at the party. If you do them ahead of time, cover each one with plastic wrap, twist the ends, and tie with brightly colored ribbon or yarn. Then you can put them in a basket for a special party centerpiece, or set one at each place for a take-home favor, if they last that long!

POPCORN ANIMALS

Mix 2 quarts (¼ cup unpopped) popped corn with 28 melted caramels. Use the sticky popcorn mixture to shape all kinds of animals. Poke in gumdrops or raisins for the eyes, nose, and mouth.

RAINBOW POPCORN BALLS

What's your favorite color? Mix a small package of gelatin dessert that comes in that color with 2 tablespoonfuls of honey and ¼ cup of melted butter or margarine. Pour the mixture over 2 quarts of popped corn, stir and toss, and make into colorful balls or any shape you choose.

PARTY PRETZELS

Make the dough for this recipe *before* your guests arrive (or if there are only two or three, they might enjoy the entire process from start to finish); then let your guests have fun shaping their own pretzels to eat hot and fresh from the oven!

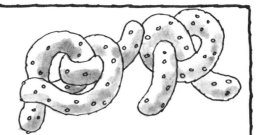

YOU NEED:

For the dough, use your favorite pretzel recipe, or a 16-ounce package of thawed frozen bread dough (white or whole wheat).

For the glaze: 1 egg white, 1 teaspoon water, coarse salt.

cover and let rise

egg white and water

salt

then bake.

YOU DO:

1. With well-floured hands, divide the dough into 20–25 pieces.
2. Roll each one into a long rope or stick; then mold them into all kinds of shapes, even the letters of your name.
3. Place all of the shapes on greased cookie sheets, leaving space between each one.
4. Cover with a damp towel for about 20 minutes so the dough can rise.
5. Finally, beat together the egg white and water and brush over the pretzels. Sprinkle with salt and pop into a 350° oven for about 20 minutes if you're using the frozen dough, or follow the directions of your recipe.

Party Gifts and Favors

There's no need to go to the store to buy birthday favors, or even gifts. Here are two ideas that can be made right at the party. They will entertain your guests and make original take-home favors at the same time!

BOTTLED SNOW

YOU NEED:

baby-food jars, one for each guest
silver glitter or bits of cut-up foil
liquid detergent
glycerine (you can buy it at your drugstore)
water
glue (optional)
old Christmas cards, magazines, postcards,
  or travel-folder pictures
crayons
tape

YOU DO:

1. Pour about a teaspoon of glitter into each baby-food jar (enough to cover the bottom).
2. Fill each jar three-quarters full with liquid detergent and a few drops of glycerine (to make the bubbles last longer). Then fill to the top with water and screw the cap on tightly. (You can add a little glue around the rim first, before tightening.)
3. Draw or cut out a winter scene and tape it to the bottle with the picture facing in.
4. Turn the bottle around, shake it up, and watch the snow fall down!

Another way: Make the jar into a paperweight by putting clay in the bottom first. You can also poke plastic figures, a sprig of pine tree, or a pinecone into the clay to make a more natural-looking winter scene.

glycerine
water
liquid detergent

Tape winter scene to back of bottle.

POP-ART PAPERWEIGHT

Here is an idea for an original birthday gift that will be sure to please your friends!

YOU NEED:

an empty food container (with label on it)
clay or Kitchen Clay (see page 82)
a laundry marker or nail polish

YOU DO:

1. Look through your pantry shelves and choose something in a can or a box that you know your friend likes to eat. Some ideas might be: a can of chicken noodle soup, powdered lemonade, peanuts; or a box of animal crackers.
2. Enjoy eating the food; then wash out the can (or shake out the box). Be sure there are no rough edges on the can (pliers will smooth them down).
3. Next, press the clay into the container, and glue a paper circle or rectangle on top.
4. Then add a personal label, like "Mack's Munchies" or "Susie's Super Soup."
5. For a pop-art effect, stick a plastic spoon or straw into a soup or drink can.
6. A brown paper sack, tied with colorful yarn, will make the perfect gift wrap.

Another tempting gift: A *pair* of weighted cans or boxes will make bookends . . . tempting enough to eat!

There are many other ideas in this book for presents or favors you can make yourself: Comic Cut-ups (p. 148), Puppetry (p. 100), Popsicle-Stick Puzzles (p. 144), Geo Board (p. 147), miniature chalkboard (p. 75), Flannel Board (p. 100), Bookplates (p. 25), "Broom Hilda" (p. 43), Ladybug House (p. 86), Autograph Hound (p. 119), and many more. See how creative you can be when planning your next birthday present.

BEAN BAGS (a game you can make and play right at the party!)

YOU NEED:

For each guest, put the following items into a plastic bag, and secure with a twisty, or a piece of yarn or ribbon:

an odd sock

dried beans or corn

a sewing needle with a large eye, threaded with colorful yarn knotted at one end (It's a good idea to tape the needle to a piece of cardboard when not in use.)

Have these items on hand for everyone to use:

scissors

felt-tip markers or scraps of fabric or felt

glue

plastic six-pack holder

cardboard

a stapler or tape

YOU DO:

1. Cut off the toe of the sock and fill it with beans or corn.
2. Fold in the ragged edges, and sew the opening securely shut with the needle and yarn.
3. Decide what your bean bag is going to be — a droopy-faced hound dog, a puffy bullfrog, a big-eyed owl, and then draw or glue on a face.
4. To make a target, tape or staple a plastic six-pack holder onto a piece of cardboard and *number the circles from 1 to 6.* (Other ideas for the targets are cardboard soft-drink cartons, cut-off milk cartons, oatmeal boxes, or tin cans with smooth edges.)
5. Play a game at your party, with each player taking turns throwing his bean bag at the target. Set a time limit and give a prize to the player who scores the most points. Everyone can take a handmade bean bag home for more target practice.

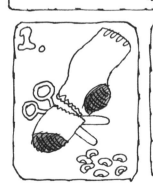
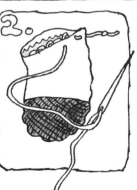

It's hard to see a party end, especially when it's your own. Playing a new kind of tag called Hug-a-Bug will give all your guests a happy send-off.

HUG-A-BUG TAG

1. Mark off a playing area indoors or out using the edges of a rug, chairs, or trees, or the driveway for the boundaries.
2. Choose one person to be the "Bugcatcher." The rest of the players, the "bugs," flit around watching for the Bugcatcher and trying not to get caught.
3. As the Bugcatcher comes near, the only way a player can avoid him is by finding another bug to hug. The two players put their arms around each other's waist and say, "We're snug as a bug in a hug. You can't catch us."
4. When the Bugcatcher calls out, "One, two, three . . . *unhug,*" all the bugs must quickly scatter and try to escape being tagged. No fair hugging the same bug twice in a row!
5. The game continues until a bug gets caught. He then becomes the new Bugcatcher.

So everyone can spot the Bugcatcher, make a *special hat* out of a mesh fruit or vegetable bag. The bugs could wear paper headbands with pipe-cleaner feelers attached.

36

A Pocketful of Birthdays

Each year at birthday time, fill a scrapbook with souvenirs from your party and other favorite things collected throughout the year. It's fun to look back at your scrapbook when you're older.

YOU NEED:

heavy paper or tagboard dividers with pockets
3-hole typing paper
pen or pencil
a 3-ring looseleaf notebook

YOU DO:

1. Save some of the following to glue onto the "party pages": wrapping paper and ribbons from your presents; invitation, guest list, and menu; headline from the newspaper on your birthday; snapshots.
2. Add a few pages of the "year's highlights," including lists of your favorite books, foods, TV programs, movies, records, and so forth.
3. Tuck some mementos into the pockets: birthday cards, a lock of hair (in a plastic bag), postcards from special trips, and anything else you've saved.

Each year add new pages and fill up new pockets so you can remember "the way it was."

Since your birthday only comes once a year, stretch it to make it last as long as possible. Instead of opening *all* your cards and family presents at once, wait and unwrap them at different times of the day. Then you'll have round-the-clock surprises.

The Birthday Child

*Everything's been different
All the day long,
Lovely things have happened,
Nothing has gone wrong.
Nobody has scolded me,
Everyone has smiled.
Isn't it delicious
To be a birthday child?*

by Rose Fyleman

GUIDE TO LEARNING CONCEPTS FOUND IN *GETTING TO KNOW AND LIKE YOURSELF*

This chapter, designed to help a child learn to know and like himself, emphasizes activities that will build and strengthen a child's self-image. Projects are presented to encourage a child to express himself — his likes, his feelings, and so on, and thereby attain a greater sense of his autonomy and his own uniqueness.

ACTIVITIES (Page)	MOVEMENT/ MOTOR COORDINATION large	small	CREATIVITY/ MAKING THINGS	LANGUAGE DEVELOPMENT/ COMMUNICATION oral/written	READING AND MATH SKILL-BUILDING	PROBLEM-SOLVING/ DISCOVERY	IMAGINATIVE PLAY/ SELF-EXPRESSION
Take a Look at Yourself (14)		X	X				
"I'm One of a Kind" (14)	X	X		X			X
Me-Doll (15)		X	X		X	X	X
"Bending Places" (16)	X	X		X	X		X
Tell without Talking (17)	X					X	X
Shadow Talk (18)	X						X
Pass the Message (19)		X				X	X
S.O.S. (20)	X					X	X
Changing Faces (21)		X	X				X
Name Nonsense (23)			X	X	X		
What's My Name? (24)				X	X	X	
Nameplates (25)		X	X		X		
Bookplates (25)		X	X		X		
Put Yourself in the Picture (26)		X	X	X		X	X
Add-a-Year Candle (28)		X	X				
Birthday Shirt (29)		X	X				
Birthday Buttons (29)		X					X
Cake Cones (30)			X		X		
Do-It-Yourself Cake Trim (31)			X			X	
Popcorn Animals; Rainbow Popcorn Balls (32)		X			X		
Party Pretzels (32)		X	X		X		
Bottled Snow (33); Pop-Art Paperweight (34)		X	X		X		
Bean Bags (35)	X	X	X		X		
Hug-a-Bug Tag (36)	X					X	X
A Pocketful of Birthdays (37)		X	X	X			

PURPLE COW TO THE RESCUE . . .
When You're Learning to Be Independent

Get into the "I can do it myself" habit by learning to do things all by yourself!

Being independent is

- zipping your jacket, buttoning your sweater, and even tying your own shoes
- hanging your raincoat on a hook so it won't fall down
- brushing your teeth the way the dentist shows you, and squeezing the toothpaste from the bottom up
- helping sort the groceries, and learning to read the labels as you go along
- surprising the family with a peanut-butter pizza and alfalfa sprouts you've grown yourself
- feeling very grown-up as you deliver an important letter to the mailbox.

Just the small, everyday successes, like pouring a cup of juice, or putting away a toy without any help, will make you feel good about yourself and more independent, too.

You're on the way to becoming independent when you've learned to dress yourself!

Practice Pal

Look for a shirt you've outgrown, or an old smock or apron, and ask a grown-up to sew on some things that will help you practice getting dressed: a zipper, a button and buttonhole, a pocket with a hankie that you can snap on, and a belt to buckle at the waist. There's no need to buy them! You can cut the zippers, buttons, hooks, and pockets off your old, worn-out clothes.

Put the shirt on a sturdy hanger, and add a face made from a paper plate. Just draw on the features and some hair, and tie or tape the plate to the hanger. Glue a photograph of yourself on the plate if you want it to look like you. Now you have a pal to help you practice getting dressed.

Another way: Make some practice pockets. Just hang up a shoe bag and put a different practice item into each pocket.

It is hard to lace and tie a shoe, but practicing on a jumbo-sized one makes it easier. You can make a *pretend* shoe with a food tray from the grocery store.

Lace It Up

YOU NEED:

crayons
cardboard or paper
scissors
paste or glue
a cardboard food tray (from fruits or vegetables)
felt-tip markers or food coloring
a shoelace

YOU DO:

1. Draw the outline of your shoe on paper or cardboard, cut it out, and glue it onto the bottom of the tray.
2. Punch three or four pairs of holes down the middle of the shoe.
3. Color *half* of a shoelace with a marking pen (or dip it into food coloring and let it dry) to show you which end to pick up next as you crisscross the laces.
4. Can you tie a bow at the top?

40

1

Round off tongue if you wish ↓

2

3

Another way: Make a different kind of practice shoe from the bottom of a plastic detergent bottle. Have an adult cut off the top, as shown in the illustration, leaving about 3 inches for the shoe. Cut two slits for the tongue and then continue from step 2, punching holes on each side next to the tongue.

Tips for Grown-ups

Think SMALL! If a child's world is *lowered* a notch or two, he'll be able to do more for himself.

A low hook or closet rod for hanging up clothes!

A mirror placed close to the floor for getting dressed.

Low shelves in the room to keep toys and books handy.

A supply of paper cups and a towel rack at a child's eye level.

A step stool to get to the things just out of reach. (You can make one from a gallon milk carton stuffed with wads of newspaper and taped shut.)

TODDLER'S SPECIAL PLACE

Another way to put things within easy reach and to help a toddler feel "included" is to set aside a low kitchen-cupboard shelf or drawer especially for him. Fill it with a few pieces of his own "cookware," like pots and pans with matching tops, some nesting jar lids, margarine tubs, plastic measuring cups, and wooden spoons. Then when you are busy mixing and stirring, broiling and baking, your young helper can be busy "cooking" too.

Hint: Hiding a surprise now and then, like crayons, clay, or a set of sponges, would really make it a special place!

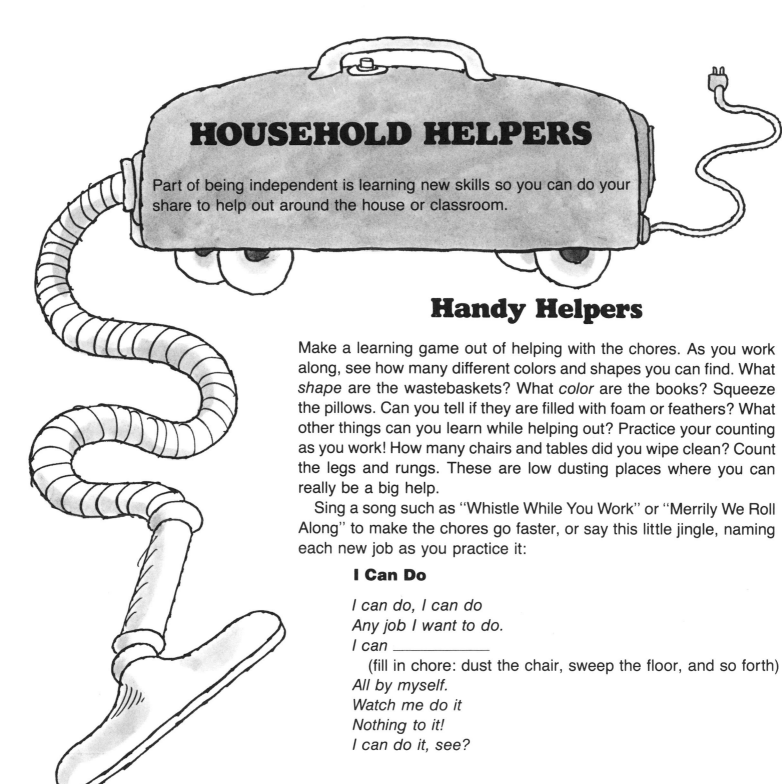

HOUSEHOLD HELPERS

Part of being independent is learning new skills so you can do your share to help out around the house or classroom.

Handy Helpers

Make a learning game out of helping with the chores. As you work along, see how many different colors and shapes you can find. What *shape* are the wastebaskets? What *color* are the books? Squeeze the pillows. Can you tell if they are filled with foam or feathers? What other things can you learn while helping out? Practice your counting as you work! How many chairs and tables did you wipe clean? Count the legs and rungs. These are low dusting places where you can really be a big help.

Sing a song such as "Whistle While You Work" or "Merrily We Roll Along" to make the chores go faster, or say this little jingle, naming each new job as you practice it:

I Can Do

I can do, I can do
Any job I want to do.
I can _____
   (fill in chore: dust the chair, sweep the floor, and so forth)
All by myself.
Watch me do it
Nothing to it!
I can do it, see?

JUNIOR DUST MOPS

To get into all those hard-to-reach places, you'll need a handy dust mop. Here are two ways to make it:

- Tie a damp rag or old diaper onto a whisk broom.
- Cut stockings into strips and tape or tie them to a paper towel or hanger tube "handle."
- Or make the tube into a "Broom Hilda" by gluing on a face, some yarn hair, and an apron fashioned from cloth scraps and ribbon; then you'll have a friendly helper to do the dusting and sweeping with you. Let "Broom Hilda" dig into the corners, behind the curtains, and under the rugs. Are you surprised to see her "skirt" getting darker and darker and darker?

←Apron

CARRYALL

A plastic pail with a handle is just right for carrying around your cleaning supplies. A cardboard soft-drink carton also makes a useful caddy. Its six sections are ready-made sorters for carrying your rags, sponges, and dusters.

Chore to Chore

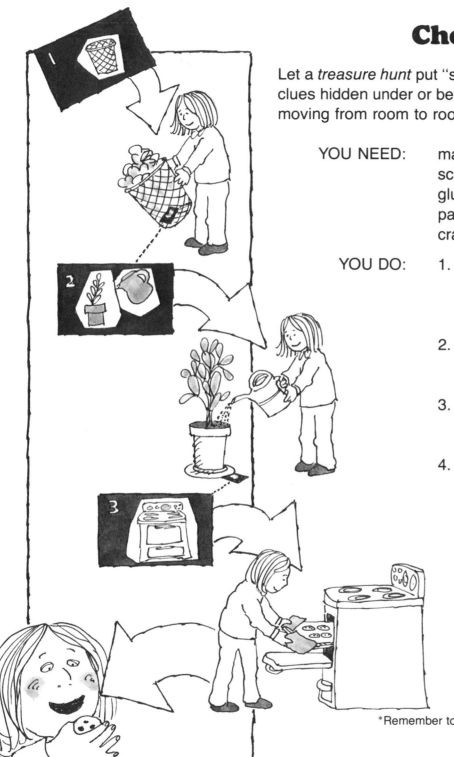

Let a *treasure hunt* put "surprises" into your cleanup routine. Picture clues hidden under or behind the places to be cleaned will keep you moving from room to room.

YOU NEED: magazine or newspaper pictures
scissors
glue
paper or index cards
crayons

YOU DO:

1. Talk about what chores need doing; then look for magazine pictures that give a *clue* to each one — a wastebasket, desk, bookshelf, jacket, pet food.
2. Cut out and glue each picture onto a card or piece of paper and number them so they can be hidden *in order*.
3. A grown-up then hides all the clues,* except the first one, which is given to you and your helpers.
4. When it's time to begin the hunt, look at clue number 1; then go where the picture tells you and see what needs to be done. If it's a wastebasket, you'll know your job is to empty it. In or under the wastebasket you'll find the *next* clue, perhaps a plant to water or a radio to dust. Continue the hunt until the *last* clue (and chore) leads you to the *treasure!* It could be an apple, a cookie, a small toy or book, or just *a big thank-you hug for the cleanup crew!*

*Remember to hide the *next* card in the place pictured on the last clue.

Chore Charts

A chart is a good way to keep track of all the ways that you're learning to help. You might not think of using an egg carton or a jar for a chart, but both will let you see and touch what you have accomplished each day.

EGG-CARTON CHART

YOU NEED:

an egg carton
glue
magazine or newspaper pictures
scissors
markers: buttons, bottle caps, dried beans, macaroni, paper circles, and so forth

YOU DO:

1. Inside the lid, draw or paste on six pictures of your daily jobs, one above each egg section.
2. Each day when you have finished a task, drop a marker into the section under the matching picture. (You can use the front row of your carton to store the extra markers.)

You could also use your egg carton to keep a *weekly* record. Mark the days from Monday to Saturday on the six egg cups. Drop in a bean each day after you finish your work, and see if the carton is filled by Sunday!

How many chores did you do today?

A JAR CHART

1. Make a set of "chore jars," pasting a picture of a job on each small container (spice, baby food, bouillon, for example).
2. As you complete a chore, drop a bean into the matching jar.

How many weeks will it take you to fill up your jars? Unscrew the lids and see how many beans are in each jar. Counting will be part of the fun of learning.

Toy Sorters

Pick up before you wind down! Anything is more fun when you make a game out of it, even cleanup time. Picking up your toys and games can be done quickly, if you have various containers for doing the sorting. *Plastic dishpans, wastebaskets,* and *laundry baskets* make ideal toy sorters. Label each container (books, trucks, blocks) to keep your large toys in order.

LARGE TOYS

For medium-sized toys, ask the ice-cream store to save some "drums." Wash them well and cover with comic strips, Contak, or wallpaper. *Tomato baskets* with handles are especially useful for puzzles and games, because you can carry them around without losing any of the pieces.

MEDIUM-SIZED TOYS

Vegetable bins or *shoe boxes* can be stacked where there's not much space. Set aside one or two bins for paint, crayons, scissors, paper, glue, tape, and other art materials. Then these basics will always be ready when you are! Your jacks, marbles, pencils, and other small items will fit nicely into a *silverware tray, muffin tin,* or *tackle box.*

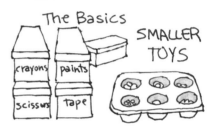

The Basics

SMALLER TOYS

A *mesh onion or orange bag* is perfect for storing bathtub toys, since it lets them "drip dry." What else can you turn into a toy sorter?

BATHTUB TOYS

Closing Up Shop

Use your imagination! Each day, pretend you are a *different* worker winding up the day. You could be a waitress cleaning up a restaurant, a mailperson sorting out the letters in the post office, an airline steward straightening up after the plane has landed, or the cleanup crew at work after a ball game. A *special hat* can put you right into the part.

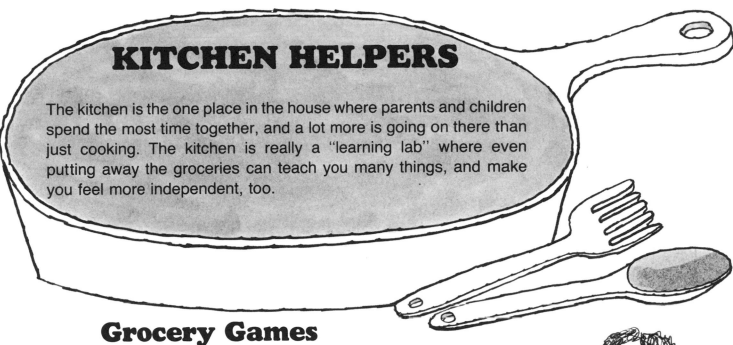

KITCHEN HELPERS

The kitchen is the one place in the house where parents and children spend the most time together, and a lot more is going on there than just cooking. The kitchen is really a "learning lab" where even putting away the groceries can teach you many things, and make you feel more independent, too.

Grocery Games

Before you put away all the groceries, save a few cans and boxes; then with some empty paper bags and a crayon or two, you'll be all set to play some grocery games!

1. First, you can *trace* around the cans and boxes and *color* in the shapes you've made. How many circles, squares, and rectangles do you have?
2. Take a second look at the containers. Do the foods come in different colors, sizes, and weights? Which is heavier: a bag of potato chips or a can of soup?
3. Now *sort* the groceries, first by category (fruits, meats, vegetables, cereals), and next by their containers (the metal ones, cardboard, plastic, and so forth). Which ones are for breakfast, lunch, dinner, and snack time?
4. When you're finished, find out where each one is kept (pantry, refrigerator, freezer, or laundry room), and put them all away!

LABEL LOTTO

Learning to "read" labels is an important step in becoming an independent shopper.

YOU NEED:

For each player, four pairs of matching labels from empty boxes, bottles, and cans (To remove the labels from bottles or cans, soak in warm water and then blot dry on a paper towel.)

cardboard, construction paper, or grocery bags for the playing boards and cards

pencil or crayon

glue

scissors

YOU DO:

To make the *lotto board* (one for each player):
Draw lines to divide the cardboard into four sections and glue a different label onto each.

To make the *playing cards:* Glue corresponding labels onto squares of construction paper.

TO PLAY THE GAME:

1. First deal out the lotto boards.
2. Next put all the cards facedown in a pile, and take turns drawing, one at a time.
3. If you draw a card that is the same as one on your board, place it over the matching picture; return the cards that don't match to the bottom of the pile.
4. The first player to cover his board is the winner.

You could also play this *all by yourself* with one lotto board.

LABEL CONCENTRATION

Make four to twelve matching pairs of label cards. Mix them up and lay them facedown in several rows. The first player turns over *two* cards. If they match, she keeps the pair and chooses two more cards; if not, she turns the cards facedown (in exactly the same place) and the next person takes his turn. The player who has the *most* pairs at the end of the game is the winner.

JUNIOR SHOPPING LIST

YOU NEED:

paper and pencil
grocery ads from the newspapers
cardboard
scissors
glue
crayons

YOU DO:

1. First go through your refrigerator and cupboards with Mom or Dad and help make a list of the food and supplies the family needs.
2. Then choose the ones you like best and make your own list by cutting out pictures from the grocery ads — or draw them yourself.
3. Glue the food cut-outs onto a piece of cardboard, including the printed name and price of each item. Color them if you wish.
4. Take your "picture list" to the store to help you pick out your groceries.
5. While you are shopping, look for some of the healthy new snack foods. Did you discover any carob-coated yogurt bars, trail mixes, wheat germ, or Tiger's milk?

Could you find everything on your list? Were the prices for each item higher, lower, or the same as the ones printed on your card?

SHOPPING SLATE

This is a shopping list that you can wipe off and use over and over again.

1. Find a piece of heavy plastic, fold it in half, and tape it shut on two sides.
2. Slip a paper, listing your basic grocery items, into the open side.
3. Then each week, just check off what you need right on the plastic with a washable marking pen (or felt-tip marker).
4. After your grocery trip, wipe off the marks with a sponge and you'll be ready to start again.

MEALTIME

TRACE 'N' PLACE

Setting the table is a daily job that's just right for you. Once you've learned how, you can do it by yourself and be a big help at the busy dinner hour. As you set the table, you'll be learning about what things go together and where they go — left, right, next to, or above. You'll be *counting* the number of forks, spoons, cups, plates and *sorting* them too. For this mealtime lesson, *you'll* be your own teacher.

YOU NEED: sheets of construction paper (12 inches by 18 inches)
crayons
a place setting: plate, spoon, fork, knife, glass or cup, napkin

YOU DO:
1. Have a grown-up help you set the silverware, glass, and plate on a piece of construction paper, putting everything where it belongs.
2. Next *trace* around each item with a crayon.
3. Then take everything off and repeat the process on more sheets of paper to make a mat for everyone in your family.
4. Now decorate all the placemats.
5. If you want to use your "practice" placemats more than once, glue them on a sturdy cardboard backing, then cover the front with clear Contak paper.

Another way: Spread a large piece of oilcloth or vinyl on the table and, with a laundry marker, carefully trace the outlines of the place settings directly on the cloth.

NAPKIN RING

You can also make a *napkin ring* to go with each placemat by cutting circles from a cardboard tube or plastic six-pack holder, or by using large curtain rings. Decorate each ring differently so everyone will recognize his own — draw or paint on a name, glue on macaroni, wrap with yarn or crepe paper, mark with stripes or holiday shapes.

Cooking or baking all by yourself, or with just a little help, will surely make you feel independent. Eating something *you've* made is always a treat, but you'll really feel proud when someone *else* asks for "seconds."

Do-It-Yourself Snacks

Here are some recipes for healthy snacks that are all easy to make.

PANTRY SNACK MIX

YOU NEED:
½ cup toasted sesame seeds
1 cup crunchy cereal
1 cup raisins
1 cup chopped dried apricots
1 small package chocolate or carob chips
1 cup chopped walnuts

YOU DO:
1. Pour all ingredients into a large bowl and mix well. (This recipe makes a big quantity, but it will last a long time if you keep it tightly covered.)
2. Be inventive. Make up your *own brand* by using any combination of seeds, cereals, dried fruits, and nuts that you enjoy.

51

PEANUT-BUTTER BALLS

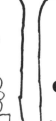

YOU NEED:

¼ cup honey
¼ cup peanut butter
½ cup oatmeal
¼ cup raisins
½ cup shredded coconut
¼ cup toasted sesame seeds

YOU DO:

1. Mix the ingredients together and form into 1-inch balls.
2. Wrap in plastic or keep in a covered container in the refrigerator.

CRISPY CHEESE SNACKS

YOU NEED:

¾ cup margarine
½ cup all-purpose flour
1 cup shredded sharp cheddar cheese
1½ cups Rice Krispies

YOU DO:

1. Beat margarine and flour until the mixture holds together.
2. Mix in the cheese and Rice Krispies.
3. Shape into small balls and place on a greased baking sheet.
4. Bake in the oven at 400° until brown (about 12 minutes).

TOAST CUPS

YOU NEED:

thinly sliced bread with crusts removed
butter
filling, such as jam, grated cheese, peanut butter and honey, chopped apples sprinkled with cinnamon and sugar or mixed with raisins or butter
muffin tin

YOU DO:

1. Flatten the bread with a rolling pin or your hands, and then spread *both* sides with softened butter.
2. Press each slice into a muffin tin section to form a cup shape.
3. Toast in a 350° oven for about 20 minutes or until the cups are crisp and brown.
4. Fill with jam, peanut butter, and so forth, and pop back into the oven for a minute or two (apples will take longer to bake).

BANANA BITES

Dip banana slices into honey, then roll them in wheat germ or ground nuts. Stick in a toothpick and eat. (Wheat germ can be found in your grocery or health-food store.)

honey   wheat germ

FRUIT POPS ON STICKS

Pour fruit juice into an ice-cube tray. When almost frozen, poke a Popsicle stick into each one. When completely frozen, unmold and pop into your mouth!

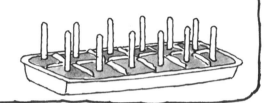

QUICKIE CHEESES

There are so many things — from snacks to desserts — that can be made with cream cheese or any other cheese. Soften the cheese (mix with a little milk in a bowl and mash with a fork) before putting together any of these tasty combinations:

1. Cheese Spread: Spread the softened cheese on pieces of celery or graham crackers.
2. Fruit Salad: Form cream cheese into balls and put them into peach or pear halves. Top with shredded cheese (such as cheddar) and serve on a bed of lettuce.
3. Jell-O Balls: Roll small cream-cheese balls in crushed nuts and add to Jell-O when almost set.
4. Cheese Kabobs: Stick cheese balls or cubes on toothpicks along with chunks of fruit, ham, olives, and so forth.
5. Triangles and Blankets: Spread the cheese between three pieces of bologna or salami, cut them into quarters, and serve the triangles on toothpicks; or spread on lunch-meat slices and roll into blankets.

53

Do-It-Yourself Meals

Follow these easy recipes and with just a little help you can make an entire meal yourself. Here are some sample menus to help you plan your meals.

☀ SUNDAY ☀ SUPPER
- Anything Soup
- Pocket Sandwich
- Yogurt Sundae

☀ LUNCH
Gelatin Salad
Peanut butter pizzas
Dress-up Pudding

☀ BREAKFAST
Juice
Banana Bites
Pancake Shape-Ups
Milk or Cocoa

ANYTHING SOUP
Anything goes in this homemade soup!

1. Start your soup stock in a big kettle by adding chicken or beef bouillon cubes to boiling water (two cubes to each quart).
2. Wash, peel, and cut up all your favorite vegetables: celery (with tops), carrots, potatoes, turnips, onions, green peppers, tomatoes, parsley, beans, and peas. Then spoon the vegetables into the kettle, being careful not to splash.
3. Add some macaroni, barley, or corn to make the soup hearty.
4. Don't forget to search the refrigerator for leftovers, including scraps of meat, to add to your soup.

5. Toss in a bay leaf, some peppercorns, and herbs, like basil, oregano, thyme, or marjoram, if you wish.
6. Simmer covered for 30 to 45 minutes.

Every good cook samples the broth as he goes along, but watch out, or there'll be nothing left for the rest of the family!

PEANUT-BUTTER PIZZAS

Spread peanut butter on toasted English muffins; then top them with some of these ingredients: jelly, honey, apple or banana slices, raisins, dry cereal, bacon pieces. Pop under the broiler, or eat as is.

POCKET SANDWICHES

Ask your grocer to help you find *pita bread* (a round flat bread with a hollow center that comes from the Middle East). Cut each piece in half and you'll have two half moons with "pockets." Stuff each one with your favorite sandwich filling, wrap in aluminum foil, and heat in a 350° oven for about 10 minutes.

POCKET STUFFINGS:

cheese slices with tuna, ham, or chicken salad
crumbled bacon bits mixed with shredded cheese
cooked hamburger, cheeseburger, or sloppy joes
leftover roast beef with gravy or barbecue sauce

PANCAKE SHAPE-UPS

Anyone can serve round pancakes for breakfast or dinner, but everyone will flip for these unusual shapes.

1. Follow the directions on your favorite pancake mix.
2. Pour the dough into a baster and then squeeze out a design, an initial, or even your name.
3. To make animal or holiday shapes, place metal cookie cutters directly on the greased pan. Once the griddle is hot, pour a little batter inside each one, leaving enough room for the pancake to rise. (An adult can remove the cookie cutters with kitchen tongs.)

MIXED-UP GELATIN SALAD

YOU NEED:

1 small package of flavored gelatin

¾ cup of boiling water

1 cup of fruit juice (orange, apple, lemon, pineapple, and so forth — match it to the flavor of your gelatin or mix it up)

2 carrots, grated

raisins, banana slices, celery bits, nuts, and so forth

YOU DO:

1. Place the gelatin in a bowl and, with an adult's help, slowly pour in the boiling water. Stir until dissolved, then add the fruit juice.
2. Mix in the grated carrots and any or all of the fruit, vegetables, and nuts.
3. Pour the gelatin mixture into six small containers or paper baking cups placed in a muffin pan.
4. Refrigerate for several hours or overnight.

JIFFY DINNERS

Did you know you can make your own TV dinner? At the end of the week, look in the refrigerator for some tasty leftovers and spoon them into recycled aluminum trays. (The partitioned kind are best, but you can make your own dividers with folded strips or "pouches" of foil.) Try to put together a well-balanced meal like meatloaf, corn, and applesauce. Cover tightly with foil and store in the freezer. Then one night when you're "in charge," just pop the tray into the oven (350° for 15–20 minutes) and dinner will be ready in a jiffy!

Dessert Time

DRESS-UP PUDDING

1. Follow the directions on a package of *instant* pudding.
2. Line small bowls or custard cups with vanilla wafers or graham crackers; then spoon some pudding into each one.
3. Dress them up with chunks of fruit, carob bits, or some chopped nuts.

Another way: Make two different flavors of pudding and layer them in a large bowl or individual parfait glasses. Push a spoon handle to the bottom, give it a "swirl," and you'll have a quick, fancy dessert. A dab of whipped topping will make your pudding even more special.

YOGURT SUNDAE

Sprinkle dry cereal over plain or frozen yogurt. Top with fresh berries, bananas, or hot-fudge sauce. (Yum.)

Cooking the Metric Way

Get ready for metric measurements. Soon all recipes will use them. No more pints, quarts, or gallons — and *no* fractions, like ¼ teaspoon or ½ cup to confuse you; just one basic unit for liquids and solids, the LITER. Although there will be new cooking utensils to make it easier, here is a table to help you switch to metrics.

240 milliliters = about 1 cup
120 milliliters = about ½ cup
15 milliliters = 1 tablespoon
5 milliliters = 1 teaspoon

(A LITER = 1000 MILLILITERS)

Have fun practicing your metric measuring with this peanut butter "fun dough" recipe.

YOU NEED: 120 ml peanut butter
120 ml honey
240 ml powdered milk

YOU DO: Mix it, knead it, play with it. Wash your hands before you begin because you may even want to *eat* it!

Another way to practice metrics is to use a simple balancing scale that you can make yourself.

BALANCING SCALE

Make the scale with a coat hanger, string, and two plastic food containers (like margarine or cottage-cheese tubs).

1. Punch four holes in the circular rims of the two containers, where the numbers 12, 3, 6, and 9 would be on a clock.
2. Tie each of the containers to the ends of the wire coat hanger with strings cut the *same length.*
3. Hang the scale on a towel rack in your kitchen, or on a closet rod, coat hook, or clothesline.

← strings cut the same length

Now *compare* the weights of different foods of the *same* quantity. For example, using a metric measuring cup, pour 240 milliliters of rice into one side of the scale and 240 milliliters of water or flour into the other. Which is heavier?

Other ways: Before you weigh anything, try to predict the results. Experiment with lots of different liquids and solids, and see if you can guess which ones will tip the scale. Now experiment with different *quantities,* trying to *balance* the two sides of the scale.

OUTDOOR HELPERS

You can learn to be independent outdoors too! Open the back door and take a good look. There you'll find a yard or playground full of things that you can do by yourself, like washing your bike or the family car, digging up weeds, watering the garden, or raking a pile of leaves high enough to jump into.

The leaves have let go and scattered about,
A hundred, a thousand, too many to count.
Rake them all up in a great big heap—
No one's looking? Come on, let's leap!

Be a Vegetable Gardener

Watching something that you have planted yourself pop out of the ground is really exciting. You not only *see* your plants grow, but you can eat them too. Give your plants a "head start" by putting the seeds into containers and letting them sprout indoors first, before transplanting them into the garden. Here's how:

YOU NEED: paper cups, clay pots, or an egg carton
                     dirt or potting soil
                     a spoon
                     packets of seeds (carrots, radishes, beans, mustard, and cress all give quick results)
                     Popsicle sticks
                     felt-tip marking pen
                     small watering can

YOU DO:

1. Poke a hole for drainage in the bottoms of each section of the egg carton or in each paper cup, or use a clay pot. Set a saucer (or the egg-carton lid) underneath to catch the water.
2. Spoon dirt or potting soil into your container.
3. Then follow the directions for planting given on the seed packet.

4. To remember what you planted, write the name of each vegetable on a Popsicle stick and poke it into the soil.
5. Water gently, every day at first; later, only when the soil is dry.
6. After the shoots are about two inches high, thin out the plants so that only one or two sprouts remain in each cup.
7. When the plants grow too large for the container, put them in your garden or into larger pots.

If there is not enough space for a real garden, you can fill pots with flower, vegetable, and herb seeds, like thyme and basil, and place them in a sunny spot outdoors or on a windowsill. Which of your homegrown vegetables or herbs would taste good in your Anything Soup (p. 54)?

GARDEN EXPERIMENTS

Gardening time is learning time too. Use your meter stick and measuring cup to find out some of the answers to these questions. Mark them down on a "growing chart."

Which seeds sprouted the quickest?
How high did the plants grow?
How many days did it take for green tomatoes to appear?
How many liters of water does your watering can hold?
How many times did you need to fill your can each day?

What else can you measure in your garden?

QUICK ALFALFA SPROUTS

Here's something that needs only water, so you can grow it right at your kitchen sink. "Plant" some alfalfa seeds on Monday, and by Friday you'll be able to serve them for supper!

1. Soak seeds overnight.

YOU NEED: a handful of alfalfa seeds (mung beans, chick peas, wheat, and rye seeds also work well)
strainer or colander
large bowl

YOU DO:

1. Put the seeds in the strainer and place it in a bowl with enough warm water to cover the seeds. Let them soak overnight.
2. The next morning, rinse the seeds under the faucet, again in warm water, being careful not to move them around too much. Pour clean water into the bowl and leave the strainer with the seeds in it (covered with a paper towel if your kitchen is sunny) until dinner time.
3. Then rinse off the seeds again and leave them soaking in clean water. Do the same thing twice a day for the next day or two. Do you see any changes in your seeds?
4. By the third or fourth day, your sprouts should be about two inches long and almost ready to eat. (Don't wait for the leaves to grow, since they are bitter.) Put the strainer in a sunny spot for several hours and watch the sprouts turn green!

2. The next morning, rinse seeds in warm water. Add warm water. Cover with paper towel all day.

3. Rinse seeds again and leave in clean water overnight. Repeat twice the next day.

Another way: You can use a jar instead of a strainer. Cover it with cheesecloth, secured with rubber bands, then place the jar on its side, and follow the steps above, being sure there is enough water in the jar to cover the seeds.

4. By the third or fourth day—sprouts.

Put them in the sun a few hours and they'll turn green.

Add your sprouts to any sandwich or salad, or eat them plain for a crunchy snack.

Sidewalk Delivery Service

Taking on a really *big outdoor job* in your neighborhood, one you never thought you could do all by yourself, makes you feel pretty grown-up. You can be helpful to the whole family by running errands, like taking bundled newspapers to the recycling center; returning empty cans and bottles to the store; getting stamps at the post office; or buying the Sunday paper and coming home with the right change.

To help you make deliveries, use a wagon if you have one, or sling a backpack or laundry bag over your shoulder. You could also make your own errand bag. Here are two ways:

SIX-PACK (for carrying larger items)

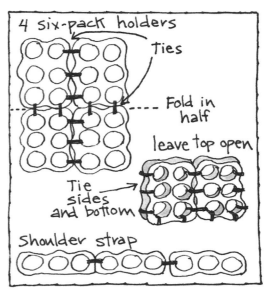

1. Collect six to eight plastic six-pack holders; then tie four of them with yarn or string. (See diagram.)
2. Fold in half and tie the two sides together, leaving the top open.
3. For a shoulder strap, cut several rows apart and tie them together.
4. Tie on a small sock to hold your loose change.

BOTTLE BASKET (for smaller items)

1. Cut off the top third of a large bleach bottle, and save it.
2. Punch holes around the edge of the bottom part of the bottle, about half an inch apart.
3. Weave yarn in and out of the holes for a colorful border.
4. Cut a strip from the top of the bottle for a handle; punch two holes at each end so you can tie the handle to your basket with yarn.

A jump rope, belt, or ribbon will also make a handle for your errand bag.

Now that you're an experienced messenger, ask the neighbors if they would like to use your delivery service, too.

GUIDE TO LEARNING CONCEPTS FOUND IN *LEARNING TO BE INDEPENDENT*

This chapter is based on the principle that a child learns to be self-confident and independent by mastering the everyday challenges in his own environment. The regular routines within the home, school, and neighborhood provide a natural setting for "self-help" activities that stimulate problem-solving, discovery, and skill-building.

ACTIVITIES (Page)	MOVEMENT/ MOTOR COORDINATION large/small		CREATIVITY/ MAKING THINGS	LANGUAGE DEVELOPMENT/ COMMUNICATION oral/written		READING AND MATH SKILL-BUILDING	PROBLEM-SOLVING/ DISCOVERY	IMAGINATIVE PLAY/ SELF-EXPRESSION
Practice Pal (40)		X	X				X	
Lace It Up (40)		X	X				X	
Toddler's Special Place (41)		X				X		
Handy Helpers (42)	X	X				X		
Junior Dust Mops; Carryall (43)	X	X	X					X
Chore to Chore (44)	X	X				X	X	
Egg-Carton Chart; A Jar Chart (45)		X	X			X	X	
Toy Sorters (46)	X	X				X	X	
Closing Up Shop (46)	X	X				X	X	X
Grocery Games (47)	X	X				X	X	
Label Lotto; Label Concentration; Junior Shopping List; Shopping Slate (48–49)		X	X	X		X	X	
Trace 'n' Place (50)	X	X	X			X	X	
Napkin Ring (51)		X	X			X		
Do-It-Yourself Snacks; Meals; Dessert Time (51–57)		X		X		X		
Cooking the Metric Way (58)		X		X		X	X	
Balancing Scale (59)		X	X			X	X	
Be a Vegetable Gardener (60)		X	X			X	X	
Garden Experiments (61)				X		X	X	
Quick Alfalfa Sprouts (62)		X	X				X	
Sidewalk Delivery Service (63)	X	X	X	X		X	X	X
Six-Pack; Bottle Basket (63)		X	X					

PURPLE COW TO THE RESCUE . . . When You're Learning the Basics to Get Ready for School

It's
- trying out some easy recipes for paint and clay
- recycling throw-aways for all kinds of creative projects
- learning new ways to use scissors, paper, crayons, and chalk
- developing your muscles, large and small, and sharpening your thinking skills
- using your five senses to practice matching, sorting, and counting.

It's each step building on the next, as you learn through play.

PAPER AND SCISSORS

Using scissors is an important basic skill that can be learned as early as age three. To get ready for cutting, move your thumb and fingers like a pair of scissors and say this verse:

Open, shut them; open, shut them,
Cutting is no trick.
Open, shut them; open, shut them,
Listen to them click.

Snap-ons

Snapping clothespins will give you more practice in moving your thumb and forefinger.

YOU NEED:

5 or 6 snap clothespins
crayons or felt-tip markers
several colors of construction paper, wrapping paper, or cloth scraps
a plastic container or box
glue

red
blue
yellow
green

YOU DO:

1. Mark a different color on each clothespin and the *matching* color around the rim of the container, as shown in the illustration. (Older children could cut out and glue on paper and cloth scraps to make the activity more challenging.)
2. See if you can clip the clothespins to the right color or pattern.
3. Now have fun unclipping the clothespins, dropping them one by one into the container, and then dumping them out again. Play the "snap-on" matching game again and again.

66

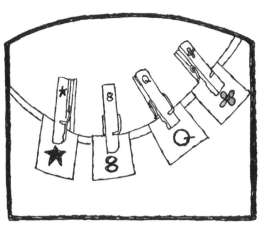

Another way:

1. Hang up a piece of clothesline or string with different numbers, letters, or pictures taped on at intervals.
2. Mark a new set of clothespins with the same numbers, letters, or pictures as those on the clothesline.

Now you are ready to use your fingers for cutting with scissors.

Snip-and-Paste Mosaic

YOU NEED:

long strips of construction paper of different widths, ½ inch and wider
scissors
cardboard food trays
paste or glue
drinking straws
yarn

YOU DO:

1. Cut the strips into pieces, starting with the narrowest ones, since they only take one snip of your scissors.
2. Paste the pieces onto the food tray to make a colorful design. Add cut-up straws and yarn to your mosaic.

67

Make a Squiggle

1. Cut paper into a circle and keep going round and round *inside* the circle, turning the paper with one hand as you cut with the other. Keep going until only a small piece is left in the center.
2. Next, hold on to the center and see what happens. Did you ever think that a small paper circle would end up looking like a coiled bed spring?
3. Push a paper clip through one end and hang up your squiggle.
4. Try cutting squiggles from some other shapes too. What designs will unfold from a square or a triangle?

Folding and Cutting

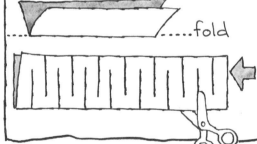

Fold a long piece of paper in half lengthwise; then mark lines on both sides to look like this. Cut along the lines and open up your paper. Do you see it "growing"?

Paper Stand-ups

1. Fold a piece of paper in half.
2. Draw an animal on it with its head at the fold and cut it out, being careful not to cut through the folded edge.
3. Put together a whole zoo or circus with your colorful animal stand-ups.

68

Stencils

YOU NEED:

cardboard
crayons or chalk
scissors
construction paper
glue

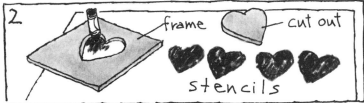

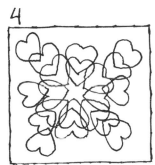

LAYERED PICTURE

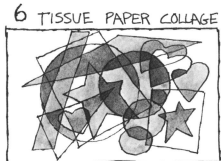

YOU DO:

1. Draw a *shape* in the middle of a piece of cardboard: a circle, triangle, heart, star, animal, etc. Ask a grown-up to help you cut out the shape. Both the cut-out part and the "frame" that is left will be your stencils.
2. Lay the stencil-frame down on a sheet of paper and color in the open space with chalk or crayon. Lift up the stencil and you will find a solid shape that will look just like your original cut-out.
3. On a new sheet of paper, try holding down the cut-out stencil with one hand and drawing around the edge with the other.
4. Move the shape around, tracing the outline each time, to create designs, in rows or in a random or overlapping pattern. (See illustration.)
5. Experiment with different colors and designs. You can make a *layered picture* by cutting out and pasting down various shapes on top of each other.
6. Older children might enjoy cutting out tissue-paper shapes to make a *collage.* Overlap several layers of shapes by brushing on white glue (thinned out with water) to keep the shapes in place. After a few minutes, brush on a top coat of glue to give your collage a shiny look.

Try this collage method to decorate a tin can or glass jar to hold flowers or pencils.

Cut a Puzzle

Here's a beginning puzzle that anyone can do, since it has just two pieces.

YOU NEED: magazines, coloring books, comic strips, or wrapping paper
scissors
cardboard
glue
clear Contak paper (optional)

YOU DO:
1. Find a simple picture from a magazine, a coloring book, comic strip, or wrapping paper.
2. Cut it out and glue it onto heavy cardboard.
3. At first, cut out only one piece with straight lines from the bottom edge. Practice fitting those two pieces back together. Later, you can cut out more pieces in simple shapes from these two pieces for a more challenging puzzle.

ZIGZAGS

 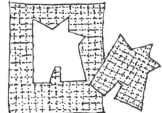

1. Take several pieces of cardboard (plain or with pictures) and cut out one or two zigzaggy shapes from *each.*
2. Mix up all the shapes and then try to match them to the correct cardboard frame.

70

PIZZA PUZZLE

1. To make a *round* puzzle, divide a cardboard pizza tray into pieces: first into just two halves, then four quarters.
2. To put the puzzle back together, lay the pieces down on another cardboard pizza tray as a guide.

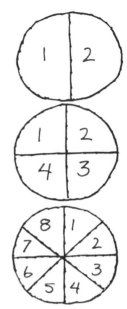

Other ways: Older children might want to make a puzzle with *more* pieces by cutting one of the quarters into eighths and the other into sixteenths (see illustration). You could also color the different parts with your crayons or markers (for example, color the half yellow; the quarters, orange; the eighths, blue; and the sixteenths, red.) Number each section, or write on the actual fractions (½, ¼, ⅛, 1/16).

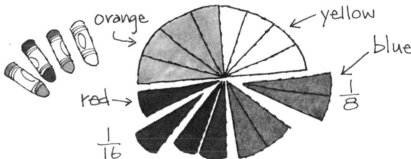

PACKAGE PUZZLE

SPONGE PUZZLE

KITCHEN PUZZLES

Your kitchen is filled with many handy supplies for puzzle-making. Empty cereal, cookie, or cracker boxes are probably the easiest to make into puzzles because the cardboard is built right in. Since you're familiar with the labels, you'll even be able to *read* your puzzle. If you cover all of the picture puzzles with clear Contak paper, they will last longer and can be sponged clean.

Puzzles are also fun without pictures. Just cut up Styrofoam trays and bright sponges to make soft, colorful puzzles.

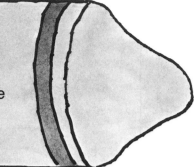

CRAYON FUN

There are so many ways to use your brightly colored crayons. Have you ever tried any of these?

Bundles

Join two or more crayons together with a rubber band, keeping the tips even; then press down and scribble away. The results may surprise you. Try some wavy lines, circles, and even your name. For variety, add more crayons and different color combinations.

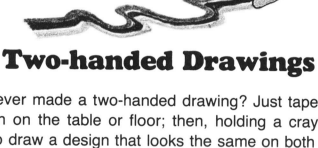

Two-handed Drawings

Have you ever made a two-handed drawing? Just tape a piece of paper down on the table or floor; then, holding a crayon in each hand, try to draw a design that looks the same on both sides. Can one hand keep up with the other?

You might enjoy doing this to music, just letting your two hands glide freely over the paper. Let the music set the mood and try keeping time with the rhythm as you draw. Does your picture look different when you're drawing to a waltz or to rock music? Can your hands keep up with the drumbeat of a marching band? Later, when you're looking at your pictures, can you match each one to the right music?

Complete your picture by coloring in the design. (You can use one hand now!)

Scratch a Rainbow

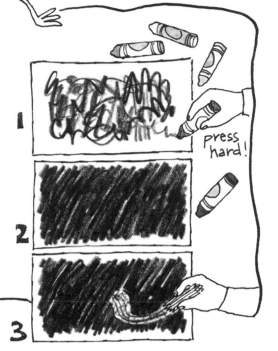

1. Pressing down hard with your crayons, completely cover a small piece of paper. Use *several* colors to make stripes or free-form designs.
2. Then cover this entire surface with a black crayon, again pressing hard.
3. Now scratch a design through the black layer with a toothpick or a Popsicle stick. What happens? Try a bundle of toothpicks. Do you see a rainbow of colors?

Magic Pictures

1. Draw a picture or a design, again pressing firmly with your crayons, this time leaving some open spaces. Then thin out some tempera paint with water and brush it lightly over your picture. Do you notice how the crayoned areas resist or stay away from the paint?
2. Now experiment with crayons and paper that *match* — draw a picture with black crayon on black paper, or green on green, and so forth. Your picture barely shows at all. Next, cover the same surface with thin white paint (or try a white crayon on white paper and cover with dark paint). Watch your magic picture appear! You can use this idea to send secret messages.

CHALK

Drawing with chalk is even easier than using a crayon but can get a bit messy. Be sure to work over newspapers or on a plastic tablecloth. If you want to save your chalk pictures, shake off the extra powder and seal with hair spray.

Did you know you can make your own chalk?

Giant Chalk Stick

YOU NEED:

2 tablespoons of powdered tempera paint
½ cup water
a small, waxed paper cup
3 tablespoons plaster of Paris
a plastic spoon or Popsicle stick

YOU DO:

1. Mix the paint and water together in the cup.
2. Slowly add the plaster of Paris, stirring with the spoon or Popsicle stick until creamy.
3. When the mixture feels hard (in about an hour), just peel off the cup and you'll have a giant chalk stick to use indoors or out.

Hint: If you dip the chalk into water first, it will slip and slide easily across your paper, and the colors will look brighter too.

Giant Chalkboard

Is there a spot in your house where you could make a giant chalkboard? How about a basement or garage wall, or the inside door of a low kitchen cabinet?

YOU NEED: masking tape
chalkboard paint or spray (sold at a paint or
    hardware store)

paintbrush
cup
sponge

YOU DO: 1. Mark off an area on the wall with masking tape; then brush or spray the paint inside the frame. (You may need several coats.)
2. Tack or tape on a cup to hold the chalk and hang up a sponge eraser with a string from a nail or a hook. (Poke a hole through the sponge first.)

sponge eraser on a string

chalk cup

Another way: To make a *miniature chalkboard,* cover a piece of heavy cardboard or Masonite with the chalkboard paint, add ribbon, rickrack, or colored tape around the border, and punch a hole to tie on the chalk and eraser.

ROLL-UP CHALKBOARD

Spray an old window shade with chalkboard paint; hang it on a window, or mount it on a strip of wood on the wall or on a closet door with brackets.

Transfer Prints

YOU NEED:

a piece of construction paper
colored chalk
a black crayon
a piece of white typing paper
a pencil or ballpoint pen

chalk drawing

covered with black crayon

typing paper

YOU DO:

1. Cover the construction paper with one or more colors of chalk.
2. Color over the chalk with a black crayon, pressing down hard.
3. To make a print, turn the paper over and place it on a piece of smooth typing paper; then draw a design on it with a pencil or a ballpoint pen.
4. Lift up the paper and see what transferred to your print. Are you surprised to see your pencil drawing in "technicolor"?

Chalk Prints

YOU NEED: string or yarn
white glue thinned with a little water
construction or newsprint paper
chalk

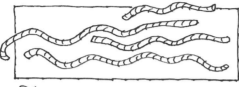

YOU DO:

1. Cut some string or yarn into pieces of different lengths.
2. Dip each one into a mixture of glue and water.
3. To make designs on the paper, let the lengths of yarn "fall" into interesting shapes (curvy, wavy, wiggly).
4. Wait until the glue is thoroughly dry (test with your fingertip), and then place another sheet of paper on top.
5. Now color all over it with the *side* of your chalk. As you rub with the chalk, watch your string design appear! Try this with crayons too.

Sidewalk Chalk

It's fun to use chalk outdoors too. Besides the usual sidewalk chalk games like Hopscotch, Foursquare, and Shuffleboard, you can also play games such as Tic-Tac-Toe and Hangman on the sidewalk.

Or try catching your shadow with chalk!

SHADOW SHAPES

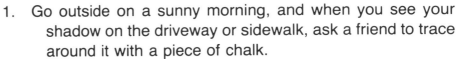

1. Go outside on a sunny morning, and when you see your shadow on the driveway or sidewalk, ask a friend to trace around it with a piece of chalk.
2. Then move to another position and outline that shadow too. Now try to fit yourself back inside the chalk lines. Don't wait until lunchtime, or you'll outgrow your shadow!

Another way: Take a *shadow walk,* looking for as many different patterns as you can find, like a tree branch or a light pole. Sketch their shapes with your chalk stick.

Back Talk with Chalk

1. Sit in a row, one behind another, facing a chalkboard.
2. The last child in line starts by *tracing* a "message" (a letter, word, shape, or number) with her finger on the back of the person in front of her.
3. That person then tries to trace the same thing on the next player's back (just like Pass the Message, page 19).
4. When the message reaches the person closest to the chalkboard, she jumps up and quickly draws it with a piece of chalk for everyone to see.
5. The player who started the "back talk" then draws what he had in mind next to it.

How has the message changed during its journey down the row? This game can be played with paper and chalk or crayons if no chalkboard is available.

PAINTING

One of the most creative of all art activities is painting. Store-bought premixed tempera paints (also called poster paints) are the best kind to use because they are thick and bright. Tempera paint in powder form is less expensive, but you have to mix it with water yourself and it tends to be runny. Here is an easy recipe that makes powdered paint work almost as well as premixed tempera.

Mix Your Own Tempera Paint

YOU NEED:

¼ cup of flour
1 cup of water
several plastic jars or cans
powdered paint (one can of each in the three
　primary colors: yellow, red, and blue)
liquid laundry starch
½ teaspoon of liquid detergent (optional)

YOU DO:

1. To make the base for the paint, put the flour in a saucepan and slowly add the water.
2. Keep stirring over medium heat for a few minutes until thick. Let cool.
3. For each different color, spoon ¼ cup of the flour *mixture* into a jar or can. Add 3 tablespoons of powdered paint, 2 table-spoons water, and ½ teaspoon of liquid starch to each. (A little detergent will make the paint shinier.)
4. Keep covered and stir well before using.

All you really need are the primary colors, red, yellow, and blue (and a jar of white paint), to make all of the other colors. Mix together yellow and blue to make green, red and blue for purple, red and yellow for orange. How would you make pink? It's best to have a separate brush for each jar of paint to keep the colors looking bright. Whether you use many brushes or only one or two, keep a can of water and a rag handy to clean them. To feel free and easy when painting, brushes with long handles are best.

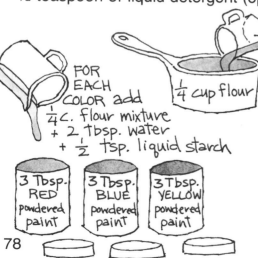

1 cup water

¼ cup flour

FOR EACH COLOR add
¼ C. flour mixture
+ 2 tbsp. water
+ ½ tsp. liquid starch

3 Tbsp. RED powdered paint

3 Tbsp. BLUE powdered paint

3 Tbsp. YELLOW powdered paint

For any "messy" art project, you'll need a smock, lots of newspapers on the worktable or floor, a sponge, and a bucket of water for quick clean-up.

Bubble Paint

For bubble paint, mix ½ cup of Ivory soap flakes and ½ cup water with tempera paint or food coloring. This thick, foamy paint will stick to milk cartons, Styrofoam food trays, and other plastic containers. Pictures painted with bubble paint will have a thick texture, almost like frosting, when dry — just right for making clouds, fluffy animals, snow scenes, trees, and so forth.

Table Easel

If you don't have an easel, it's easy to make one out of a large corrugated cardboard box. Just follow the diagram and these directions:

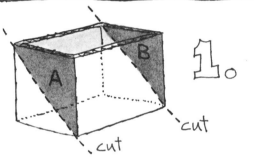

1. Have a grown-up help you make diagonal cuts along two sides of the box.
2. Fold flaps A and B in behind side C.
3. Now tape the bottom piece securely against the sides.

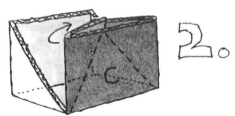

You could also use a plywood or Masonite board (sometimes called pressed wood) for an easel. Prop it up against the seat back of a kitchen chair. Then cover the seat with newspaper or plastic to hold a tray of paints, brushes, and water.

For paper, buy large pads of newsprint or save and cut up your large grocery bags — they're free! Use tape, thumbtacks, metal clips, or clothespins to attach the paper to the easel. Now you're ready to paint.

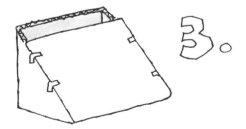

Roll-ons

Paint "roll-ons" are easy to make and fun to use. Ask an adult to help you pry off the top section of an empty plastic roll-on deodorant bottle; wash it thoroughly, fill with *thin* tempera paint, and snap the top back on. The paint will roll out in long, smooth strokes, without spilling a drop!

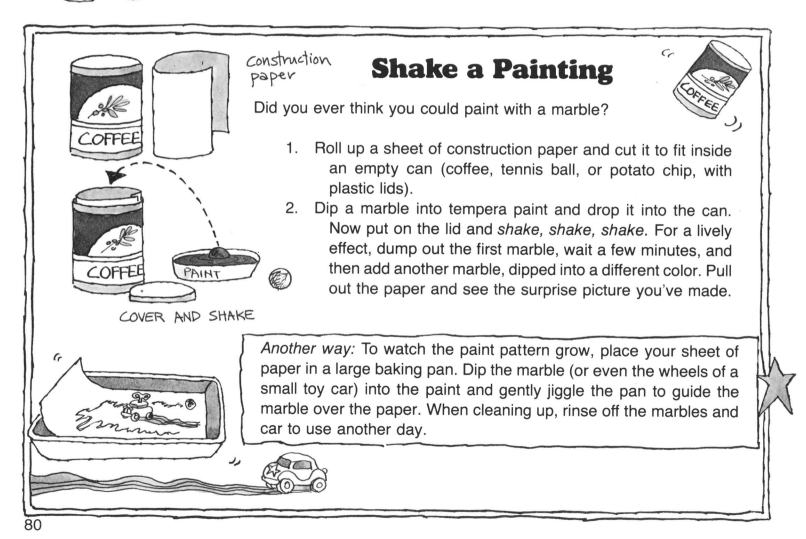

} Pry off the entire top (not just the marble).

Keep cap on when not in use.

Construction paper

Shake a Painting

Did you ever think you could paint with a marble?

1. Roll up a sheet of construction paper and cut it to fit inside an empty can (coffee, tennis ball, or potato chip, with plastic lids).
2. Dip a marble into tempera paint and drop it into the can. Now put on the lid and *shake, shake, shake.* For a lively effect, dump out the first marble, wait a few minutes, and then add another marble, dipped into a different color. Pull out the paper and see the surprise picture you've made.

COFFEE

PAINT

COVER AND SHAKE

Another way: To watch the paint pattern grow, place your sheet of paper in a large baking pan. Dip the marble (or even the wheels of a small toy car) into the paint and gently jiggle the pan to guide the marble over the paper. When cleaning up, rinse off the marbles and car to use another day.

Magic Painting Bags

Here is a novel way to finger paint without ever touching the paint!

YOU NEED:
1/4 cup of liquid laundry starch
3 tablespoons of powdered tempera paint
a large Ziploc plastic bag
masking or cloth tape
construction paper (several different colors)

YOU DO:
1. Pour the starch and tempera paint into the bag; then squeeze out the air before closing and locking it. (An extra piece of tape across the top will prevent any leaks.) Squeeze the bag gently with your fingers to blend the paint and starch.
2. Lay the bag down on the kitchen table (or your desk or a table at school). Use your fingers and hand to create one picture after another, smoothing out the bag each time you're ready to "erase" what you've done. Perhaps you'd enjoy doing this to music too!
3. For a more colorful effect, slip pieces of construction paper under your magic painting bag.

Enjoy this finger-paint recipe *without* the plastic bag too. (But don't forget to put newspapers underneath.)

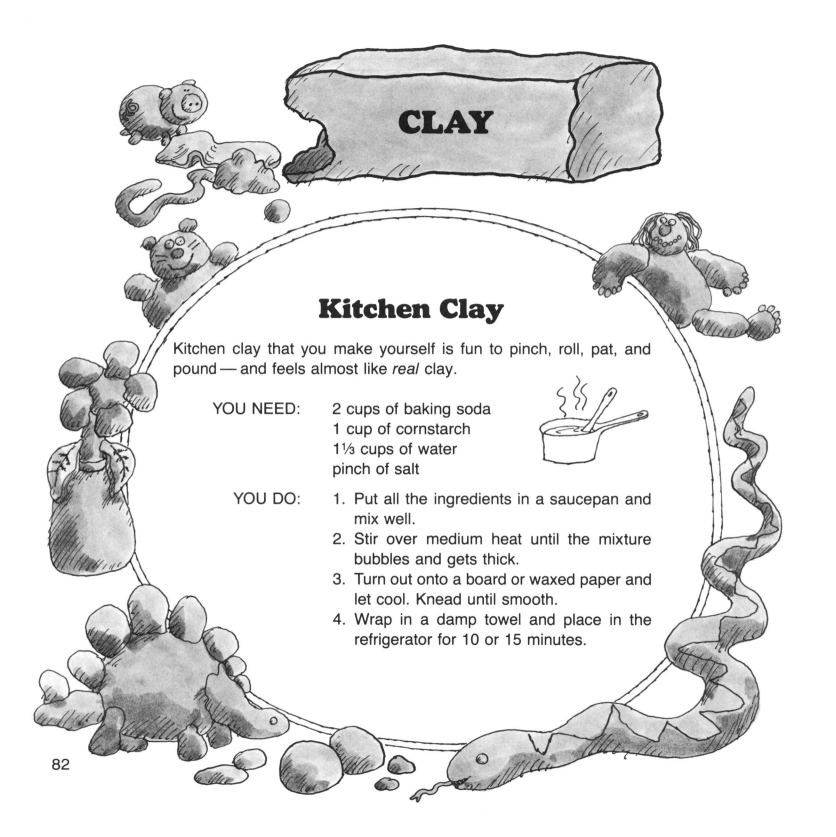

CLAY

Kitchen Clay

Kitchen clay that you make yourself is fun to pinch, roll, pat, and pound — and feels almost like *real* clay.

YOU NEED:
- 2 cups of baking soda
- 1 cup of cornstarch
- 1⅓ cups of water
- pinch of salt

YOU DO:
1. Put all the ingredients in a saucepan and mix well.
2. Stir over medium heat until the mixture bubbles and gets thick.
3. Turn out onto a board or waxed paper and let cool. Knead until smooth.
4. Wrap in a damp towel and place in the refrigerator for 10 or 15 minutes.

Ideas for Clay Play

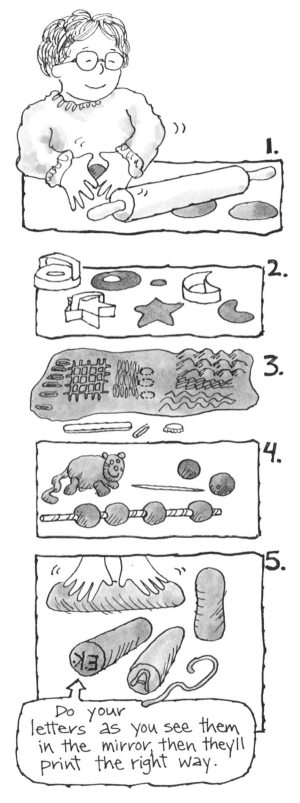

1. Roll a small piece of clay into a ball, then press it down with your palm or flatten it with a rolling pin.
2. Cut it into shapes using cookie cutters, an upside-down jar, or other kitchen gadgets.
3. Make it bumpy in lots of different ways: poke or pinch it with your fingers, roll your knuckles over it, or experiment with "tools" like a Popsicle stick, paper clip, hair roller, or bottlecap.
4. Shape it into animals, people, or beads. (Poke a hole through each bead with a toothpick or plastic straw and stack them on another drinking straw to dry.)
5. To make printing *stampers,* roll a piece of clay into a cylinder. Bang one end down to flatten it and use a stick or pencil to "etch" a design, a letter, your initials, or your name on it. (Be sure to etch letters and words backwards so they'll come out right!) You could also make a raised design on your stamp by pulling out parts of the clay or adding on small pieces. After the stamper is dry, brush on some shellac or nail polish; then it will be ready to be dipped into paint, or used with an ink pad for printing.

If you'd like to keep your other clay creations, just let them dry in the air for a day or so; then paint with tempera or acrylic paints and cover with shellac. Your unused clay can be kept soft in a tightly closed plastic bag in the refrigerator. Add a few drops of water to the bag to keep the clay from getting hard.

Do your letters as you see them in the mirror, then they'll print the right way.

Specials
du Jour
strawberries - 25¢
Fish Plate - $1.00
Pizza - $1.00
Filet Mignon $30.00

Fun-Dough Restaurant

Turn your clay-modeling talents into a unique project. Create some clay "food" and set up a pretend restaurant. The food will look real, if you add food coloring to batches of clay, or paint the hardened objects, as described on page 83.

1. You'll need a table and chairs, paper or plastic plates, cups, bowls, silverware, and napkins. Don't forget a pad and pencil and a tray!
2. Take turns being the customers, cooks, waiters, waitresses, and cashier. A few dress-up clothes will put you into the part!
3. Post a menu for everyone to see. Paste on magazine or newspaper pictures of your "specialties" (favorite foods you'll be serving).
5. Seat the customers and take their orders on your pad. Give them to the "short-order cook" in his chef's hat and apron to shape up quickly and arrange on your tray.
6. Don't let your customers leave without paying the bill. And be sure to say "thank you, come again!"

Change your "specials" to fit the season. For example: pumpkin pie in October and November; strawberries in springtime; ice cream and watermelon for summer.

84

BILL
hot dog - 50¢
Sundae - 50¢
TAX $1.00
      .50
     $1.50

Chez Fred
Restaurant
MENU
Hot Dog - 50¢
Hamburg - 55¢
French fries - 25¢
Hot fudge
Sundae - 50¢

GET IT TOGETHER

Now put all your art know-how together! You can use it to practice sorting, counting, matching, and other skills to help you get ready for school. Whether you are cutting and pasting up a costume, building a Junk Sculpture, designing a Marble Raceway, or matching a ladybug to its house, you're really learning while you're creating.

Yarn Thingamajig

Even a silly yarn thingamajig can teach you colors, matching, and measuring!

YOU NEED:

yarn
scissors
margarine tub or oatmeal carton (with a lid)

YOU DO:

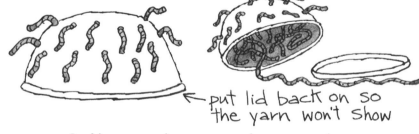

← put lid back on so the yarn won't show

1. Cut pieces of yarn of *varying* lengths and colors and poke them into holes punched all around the container. Leave exactly the *same* lengths showing on the *outside* so no one will know how long each one really is.

2. Just for fun, have everyone come up with a name for the Yarn Thingamajig. What does it look like? A shaggy dog? A shower head? A spaghetti machine? Everyone will probably see it differently.

3. Now, one by one, each person chooses a piece of yarn and pulls it out.

4. Compare the lengths to see who got the longest and the shortest. Did you pull a winner?

5. Now see how *you* measure up. Is your piece of yarn longer or shorter than your nose? Your thumb? Your foot or arm? Is it long enough to go around your "middle"? Can you put two short ones together to equal one long one?

Your Yarn Thingamajig can help you choose up sides or make decisions. Just pull the yarn to see who gets to . . .

- be the leader
- play on the red team
- start the next game
- choose today's story
- or, best of all, skip the cleanup!

Ladybug House

Ladybugs, with their built-in spots, are ready-made math teachers. Use them to practice counting, matching, and simple addition and subtraction.

YOU NEED:

an egg carton
scissors
pipe cleaners or straws
crayons or felt-tip markers
construction paper
paper punch
glue
several empty containers such as small boxes, milk cartons, corrugated light-bulb cartons, etc.

YOU DO:

1. To make "ladybugs," cut out egg-carton cups and insert pipe cleaners or cut-up straws for the feelers. On each bug, draw a different number of spots or glue on dots (made with a paper punch).
2. Construct "houses" from various containers and mark a different number on each one.
3. Now MATCH each spotted ladybug to the house with the corresponding number.

Other ways:

- If you're older, you might set up "apartment houses" by stacking several numbered containers and then adding up their total. What combinations of ladybugs can visit apartment number 8?
- Make each ladybug a different color and put a matching color on each house, or use cloth scraps or wrapping paper and match the patterns.
- Change the spots to shapes, pictures, or letters of the alphabet.

What else could the ladybugs teach you?

Dozen Down

The egg carton is ideal for making a sick-at-home or waiting game because it's a game board, counting tray, and storage box all in one.

YOU NEED: 2 dice or 2 sets of playing cards (ace to 6)
an egg carton for each player (numbered 1 to 12 inside)
12 markers per player (beans, pennies, bottlecaps)
toothpicks to keep score

YOU DO: 1. The first player tosses the dice into the lid. He then places a marker over *each* number or the *sum* of the two numbers shown on the dice. For example, if he throws a 2 and a 4, he can cover 2 and 4, or 6 — not both!

2. His turn continues as long as he can cover *both* of the numbers or their *total*. After that, the dice are passed to the next player who tries to cover the numbers in his box. *Note:* If one of the two numbers thrown is already covered, the player cannot cover the other one.
3. When a player has covered all 12 numbers in the egg cups, he calls "Dozen Down!" and pokes one toothpick into his egg carton to keep track of his score. Then another round begins.
4. When you're ready to stop, count up your toothpicks. The winner is the one with the most.

Another way: If you're just learning your numbers, use only one die, and number the cups from 1 to 6. Older children can try subtracting instead of adding.

What other egg-carton games can you think of?

Junk Sculpture

YOU NEED:

boxes and containers of all sizes and shapes
cardboard tubes
egg cartons
glue or tape
paint
crayons or felt-tip markers
construction or crepe paper
scissors
junk materials like cloth scraps, yarn, buttons, etc.

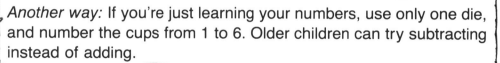

YOU DO:

1. Create animals, people, or free-form constructions by gluing or taping together all kinds of boxes, cartons, and tubes.
2. Decorate your sculpture with paint, crayons, or construction or crepe paper. Then add buttons, shells, beans, beads, cloth scraps, or whatever you've collected.

This is even more fun to do as a group project and is a good party game.

Marble Raceway

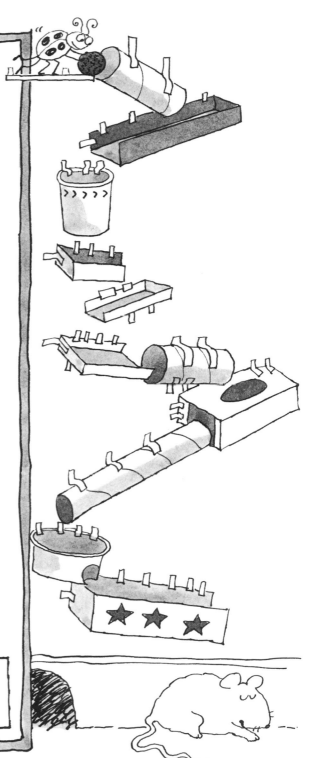

Use your new skills and some throw-away materials to construct this challenging racetrack. At the same time, you'll discover basic principles of gravity, speed, and motion.

YOU NEED:
- a large piece of cardboard, a box lid, or a blank wall
- cardboard tubes, paper cups, egg cartons, small boxes, etc.
- construction paper
- scissors
- masking tape
- marbles

YOU DO:
1. Find a suitable wall for your "raceway" or use a large piece of cardboard or a box lid.
2. Tape on tubes, boxes, long strips of folded paper, and so forth, to make the *runs.* (Be sure to construct side walls to keep the marbles from falling off the track, and build each "lane" slightly *lower* than the one before it.)
3. *Experiment* with different lengths, angles, and openings. *Design* chutes, turns, tunnels, zigzags, or jumps.
4. Now drop a marble into the opening at the top and watch gravity at work as the marble zooms, rolls, and bounces along.

Why not build two courses side-by-side and have a marble race?

Another way: Try using balls of different sizes and weights. Which will roll through the course faster, a Ping-Pong ball, a jacks ball, or a marble?

Newspaper Dress-up

You'll get plenty of practice cutting, pasting, and taping while you and your friends create newspaper fashions.

YOU NEED: two children (or a group)
newspapers
scissors
masking tape
glue
construction paper or crepe paper
saved materials (optional): paper cups, food
   trays, oatmeal cartons, egg cartons
ribbon or yarn

YOU DO:

1. Talk about what you want to be and then plan your costume (ballerina, drum major, hula dancer, king, and so forth) with your partner or team of designers.

2. Take turns being the "designer" and "model."

3. To make the basic pattern, the "designer" cuts a hole in the center of a large piece of newspaper to slip over the head; *or* places one page of newspaper on the front and one on the back of the "model," taping the two pieces together at the shoulders.

← ice cream container crown

← fringed paper beard

4. Then tape on more newspaper pages sleeves, pants, long skirts, and so forth your costume needs them.

5. Trim the outfit by gluing on crepe or construction paper and various saved materials. For example, make crepe-paper ruffles for the ballerina; fringe the newspaper for the hula dancer's skirt; dress the drum major in an oatmeal-carton hat and epaulets made of food trays. How would you make the collar and cuffs for a Pilgrim? Or a magic wand for a fairy godmother?

For a costume party or school project, have a fashion show with several "designers" telling about their models' original outfits.

GUIDE TO LEARNING CONCEPTS FOUND IN *LEARNING THE BASICS*

This chapter highlights activities which require small muscle coordination; the child actually creates his own art materials — paint, chalk and clay — and then develops his motor skills and sensory awareness as he works with them. Most of the projects are designed to help a child develop beginning readiness skills with repeated opportunities to practice using letters, numbers, lines, and shapes.

ACTIVITIES (Page)	MOVEMENT/ MOTOR COORDINATION large/small		CREATIVITY/ MAKING THINGS	LANGUAGE DEVELOPMENT/ COMMUNICATION oral/written	READING AND MATH SKILL-BUILDING	PROBLEM-SOLVING/ DISCOVERY	IMAGINATIVE PLAY/ SELF-EXPRESSION
Snap-ons (66)		X			X		
Snip-and-Paste Mosaic (67)		X	X				
Make a Squiggle (68)		X	X		X		
Folding and Cutting (68)		X	X				
Paper Stand-ups (68)		X	X				
Stencils (69)		X	X		X	X	
Cut a Puzzle; Zigzags; (70) Pizza Puzzle; Kitchen Puzzles (71)		X			X	X	
Bundles; Two-handed Drawings (72)		X	X		X	X	
Scratch a Rainbow; Magic Pictures (73)		X	X		X	X	
Giant Chalk Stick; Giant Chalkboard (74); Roll-up Chalkboard (75)		X			X		
Transfer Prints (75); Chalk Prints (76)		X	X			X	
Sidewalk Chalk (76); Shadow Shapes (77)	X	X			X	X	
Back Talk with Chalk (77)		X			X	X	
Mix Your . . . Paint (78); Bubble Paint (79); Table Easel; Roll-ons (80)		X			X	X	
Shake a Painting (80)		X	X		X	X	
Magic Painting Bags (81)		X	X		X	X	
Kitchen Clay (82)		X			X		
Ideas for Clay Play (83)		X	X		X	X	
Fun-Dough Restaurant (84)		X	X	X	X	X	X
Yarn Thingamajig (85)		X	X	X	X	X	X
Ladybug House (86)		X	X		X	X	
Dozen Down (87)		X			X	X	
Junk Sculpture (88); Marble Raceway (89)		X	X			X	
Newspaper Dress-up (90)		X	X	X			X

Purple Cow to the Rescue . . . When Traveling

Any kind of trip — a week's vacation or just a day's outing — can be an adventure. Plan ahead for that long car, train, bus, or plane ride, including some extra touches to make it more fun:

- snacks that won't melt or crumble
- a pillow or two and a favorite toy
- a few lap projects made in advance, and plenty of radio games, songs, and stories that need no materials at all
- ideas to give everyone breathing space and exercise, even though you're all jammed in together
- a few surprises tucked away that will keep the squirmers happy.

Then, instead of "Are we almost there?" or "How much longer?" you'll hear, "When can we do this again?"

Try these traveling ideas when you're on a school field trip or while *waiting* . . . at the doctor's office or at a busy restaurant. These activities will also be a lifesaver during that endless hour before supper!

GETTING READY

A Survival List

Just follow this handy checklist to make your trip go more smoothly.

Perhaps the most important reminder of all: Buckle up *everyone's* seatbelts before you start the car!

Stop home deliveries.... milk, newspaper, mail. Arrange for pets...plants...lawn. Lock doors and windows... Emergency car Kit: flashlight, flares, jumper cable, tire gauge...

- [ ] Pillows + Blankets or sleeping bags.
- [ ] Litter bag pinned or taped to the back of the front seat of the car.
- [ ] A First Aid Kit.
- [ ] Wash-up packets for sticky fingers, a box of tissues, and a roll of paper towels for lap mats.
- [ ] A Thermos or canteen of water.
- [ ] Trays, clipboard, or box lids (for "lap tables").
- [ ] A rope or ball for letting off steam during rest stops.
- [ ] An extra-long leash to exercise the pets who are traveling with you.

Take-Along Snacks

Snacks always help to pass the time when you're traveling. Here are some easy and tasty ideas for nibblers to prepare and wrap up ahead of time. Small plastic bags with twists are ideal for storing individual portions of food. Stay away from snacks that are sticky, spoil easily, or make everyone terribly thirsty.

94

Carrots and celery, beef or salami sticks, homemade granola, raisins, apples, oranges, and bananas all make nutritious food breaks. Bread sticks, melba toast, soft pretzels, and animal crackers are also popular snacks for the whole family.

If you have a cooler or a Styrofoam chest, you can also bring along hardboiled eggs, sandwiches, cheeses, cut-up fruits and vegetables. Cubes of meat and cheese can be stacked on toothpicks for handy individual servings.

Trip Tape

Making a trip tape before you leave will help you learn about places you'll see along your travel route. Once you're on your way, this activity will keep everyone busy marking off the miles.

YOU NEED:
a map of the travel area
adding-machine tape or narrow paper strips
   glued or taped together
pencil or pen
cardboard toilet-paper tubes
paper punch (optional)

YOU DO:

1. Look at a road map and mark your travel route; then list on the tape the names of the cities, rivers, and other landmarks along the way.
2. Later, as you pass each town or landmark, unroll the tape and punch a hole or make an "X" to mark off the miles!
3. Store your tape inside a cardboard tube until trip time.

Tip: If you're going back the same way, reroll the tape so that the end is now the beginning. Now you can *see* where you have been and how far you still have to go.

THINGS TO MAKE AHEAD

As the departure day grows closer, do-it-ahead activities will involve the whole family in the excitement. If you take time to make these basic toys and games *before* you leave, you can relax and enjoy them once you're underway. And best of all, the games can be used again and again, long after the trip is over.

Pretend Driving

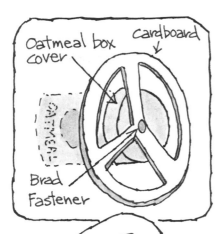

The younger passengers will enjoy having their own junior steering wheel.

YOU NEED:
- cardboard
- an oatmeal box
- brad paper fastener
- hanger tube
- scissors

YOU DO:
1. Cut out a large cardboard circle and attach it to the lid of an oatmeal box with a brad fastener; replace the lid on the box.
2. Poke a small hole in the side of the box and push a hanger tube through to use as a gear shift.
3. Holding the oatmeal box between your knees, take turns steering and giving directions: "We're coming to a railroad crossing, slow down and shift gears"; "Turn left"; "Here's a curve"; "Stop at the light."

Magic Peepers

YOU NEED: plastic six-pack holder cut into pairs of rings, or two connecting egg-carton cups with the centers cut out
cellophane of various colors
scissors
glue or tape
yarn

YOU DO:

1. Cut the cellophane into circles slightly larger than one six-pack ring or egg cup.
2. Glue or tape the cellophane circles onto the rings or egg cups.
3. Attach yarn on each side to tie around your head. (You'll need to poke holes in the egg cups for the yarn.)
4. Use your "magic peepers" to watch the world go by through different colored lenses.

Another way: You could also peep through a telescope: just cover one end of a cardboard tube with cellophane.

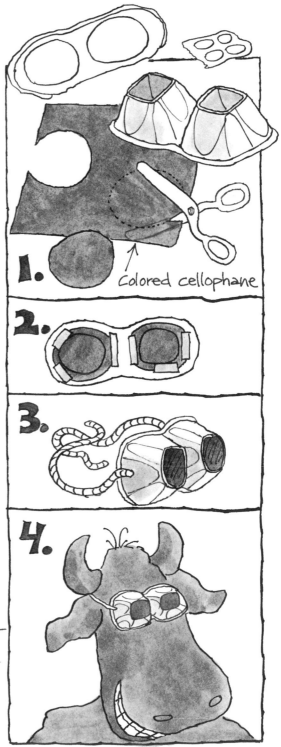

1. Colored cellophane

2.

3.

4.

Purple Cow Bingo

YOU NEED: pieces of cardboard (one for each player)
crayons or felt-tip markers
glue
magazines or newspapers (optional)
scissors

YOU DO:

1. Make a game board for each player. Mark off 9 squares on pieces of cardboard and, in the center square of each, draw a Purple Cow for a "free" square.

2. On the remaining 8 squares, draw or glue on names or pictures of things you might see during your trip, such as a painted van, a giant water tank, a billboard, or a drive-in movie. Be sure no two boards are exactly alike. (You can use the same pictures but be sure they're in different squares.)

3. Each time you spot something that is pictured on your card, call out, "I spy a _____," and mark an "X" on it. Anyone else who sees the same object can also cover it. (Of course the Purple Cow is "free.")

4. The first player to get a row of "X"s calls out "Purple Cow."

5. Play this game over and over again by trading cards and changing your "mark" or the color of your crayon.

98

Keep-Busy Box

Fill a shoebox or a small suitcase with lots of household objects to keep your carload of travelers interested for hours. Find things to touch, turn, sort, count, look at, listen to, and investigate:

- a mirror for making funny faces and watching finger puppets perform.
- a door latch, lock and key, and nuts and bolts to tinker with
- a magnet and many small items (metal and nonmetal) to try picking up: paper clips, coins, buttons, bobby pins, rubber bands, and so forth
- a magnifying glass to explore everything around you
- assorted unbreakable jars and bottles with matching lids to screw on and off
- a mesh bag from oranges and onions and some yarn (with tape wound around one end to make a point) for weaving
- a "miniature chalkboard" (p. 75) and chalk — wonderful traveling companions for writing, drawing, and playing guessing games.

Use sandwich bags, envelopes, or small boxes to keep the various toys sorted. You can make everything easy to find by attaching each toy to a piece of heavy cardboard with rubber bands or elastic knotted on the back. (See illustration.)

To make each activity a surprise, wrap the toys and games in newspaper, comic strip, or tissue paper tied with yarn.

Flannel Board

A miniature flannel board is fun to play with when traveling or waiting.

1. Just glue a piece of felt or flannel onto the lid of a small box, such as a shoe box.
2. Make felt cut-outs for storytelling, counting, or practicing words and letters. Magazine pictures mounted on cardboard will also stick to the flannel if you glue a piece of sandpaper or press rolled masking tape on the back.
3. Store the cut-outs inside the box to use on your next trip.

Puppetry

Puppetry is ideal for the car since a whole cast of characters can travel with you (and take up very little extra space).

BOX-LID PUPPET THEATER

YOU NEED:

a sturdy box lid
construction paper
scissors
crayons or felt-tip markers
Popsicle sticks, straws, or tongue blades
glue
yarn
crepe paper

YOU DO:

1. Using the box lid for a stage, make several backdrops for scenery out of construction paper. (Just trace around the lid to get the right size.) Draw or cut and paste on construction-paper clouds, trees, buildings, furniture, a sandy beach or forest, and so forth, changing the background to fit the story.

100

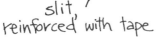

slit,
reinforced with tape

2. Make simple stick puppets by attaching paper or cardboard cut-outs to Popsicle sticks, straws, or tongue blades. Glue on yarn hair and crepe or construction paper clothes. (You can also create pets, cars, bicycles, and other props to "perform" on your stage.)

3. Cut a slit along the bottom edge of the lid and reinforce with tape, so you can slip your puppets in when it's time for the show. They will come to life when you move them back and forth across the stage!

4. Store the scenery and puppets in the box until trip time.

Who will your puppets be? Will you choose a favorite storybook, comic strip, or TV character?

FINGER PUPPETS

Finger puppets make an entertaining "road show" and all the makings will fit into a small bag.

1. Cut out construction-paper circles or egg-carton cups for the heads, or use Styrofoam or old Ping-Pong balls with a hole poked in for your finger.

2. Draw on faces and hair with felt-tip markers or crayons (or glue on yarn and paper features).

3. Attach the heads to your fingers, using tape if necessary.

Of course you don't really need anything but a pen to make finger puppets right on your fingertips.

POP-UP PUPPETS

I'm the perfect traveling companion you see —
No curtain or stage is needed for me
'Cause I pop up
Right out of a cup!

YOU NEED:

egg-carton section (one cup)
1 paper cup
crayons
yarn
construction paper
cotton
glue
straw or Popsicle stick
tape

YOU DO:

1. Draw a face on an egg-carton cup.
2. For hair, ears, whiskers, and a hat, glue on yarn, paper, cotton, and so forth.
3. Poke a hole and push the straw or Popsicle stick through the egg cup, taping it securely inside. (See illustration.)
4. Now poke a hole in the bottom of the paper cup and put the other end of the straw or Popsicle stick through it.
5. Push the straw or stick up and down and your puppet will *pop up* and talk to you.

Each traveler can have a different puppet — the back of the seat makes the perfect stage.

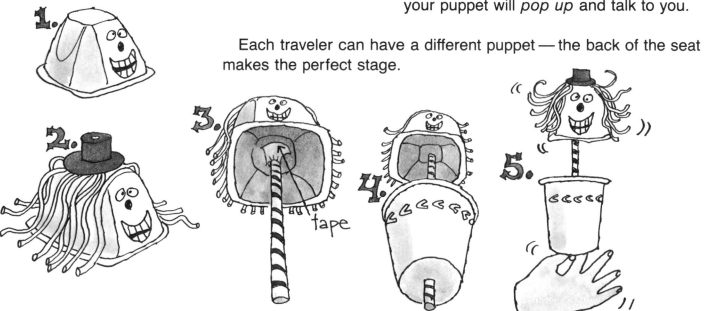

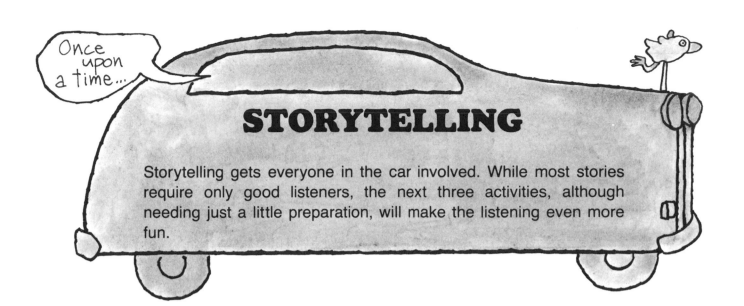

STORYTELLING

Storytelling gets everyone in the car involved. While most stories require only good listeners, the next three activities, although needing just a little preparation, will make the listening even more fun.

Story Fill-ins

Make up several story outlines and write them down before you leave. Then fill in the blanks as you go along, using your imagination and sense of humor. Adding sound effects while you tell the stories together will make it even more fun. EXAMPLE:

Our Trip

One day _____ and _____ decided to take a trip to visit _____. As we rode along we told funny stories about _____ and _____ and everybody giggled (sound effects). That night we stopped at a motel and knocked on the office door (knock, knock). We soon turned the key in the lock on our room and laughed when we saw a _____. I took a shower (sounds) and sang _____. Then next day we spotted a funny sign on the road that said _____ and a water tank on which someone had painted _____. The craziest thing that happened to us that day was _____.

It's fun to tell the same story over and over, each time putting in new names and places.

Traveling Tales

YOU NEED:

a drawstring bag (a plastic shopping or tote bag) filled with small odds and ends collected around the house:

old pair of glasses
mirror
glove
dangle earring
balloon
kitchen timer or a wristwatch with a second hand
button
silk scarf
perfume bottle
special ribbon or artificial flower
buckle

YOU DO:

1. The first player reaches inside the bag, pulls something out, and begins telling a story about it: "Once upon a time a boy found a belt buckle." You might spark fantasy stories by pretending that some things are magic — "the king's jeweled buckle," or "a crystal bottle where the genie lives."

2. After a minute or two on the timer, the first storyteller passes the bag on to the next player who *continues* the story by weaving it around whatever he has drawn from the bag. He might begin with "One day . . ."

Another way: You can also pass around the *same* object from player to player, making up a continuous story about it. In either case, let your imagination grow with the story.

Why not play Traveling Tales with your Flannel Board? Pass it from lap to lap, adding a new felt cut-out as you add on to the story.

RADIO FUN

Many travel activities require no preparation, just your ingenuity and what's around you. A good example is the car radio that can inspire instant family fun.

What's Next?

Before turning on the radio, try to guess what you'll hear: a man's or woman's voice; the weather forecast; the score of a ball game; fast or slow music, and so forth. Change the stations so you can guess some more. Now listen to one station carefully and try to imitate what you hear.

Radio Word Game

Assign each person a word that you often hear, such as "mister," "today," or "hello," and see whose word comes up first on the radio. Then try another game — count how often you hear a word within a given time limit.

Name the Tune

Turn on a music station and listen for a few seconds. Quickly turn down the volume and see who can be the first to name the tune or sing the rest of the song. If no one recognizes the music, play the radio a bit longer and guess again — or try another station. Can you name the pop singer or rock group whose record is being played?

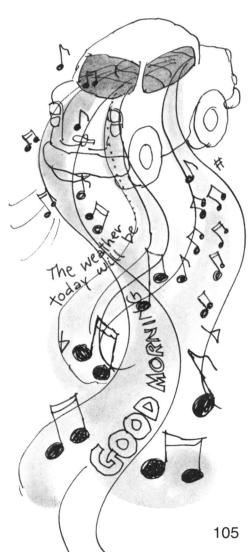

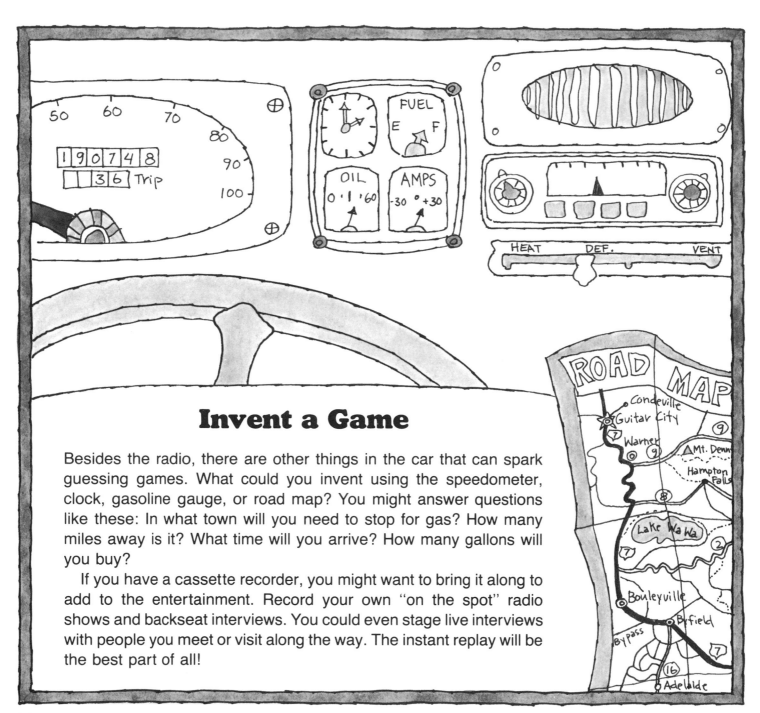

Invent a Game

Besides the radio, there are other things in the car that can spark guessing games. What could you invent using the speedometer, clock, gasoline gauge, or road map? You might answer questions like these: In what town will you need to stop for gas? How many miles away is it? What time will you arrive? How many gallons will you buy?

If you have a cassette recorder, you might want to bring it along to add to the entertainment. Record your own "on the spot" radio shows and backseat interviews. You could even stage live interviews with people you meet or visit along the way. The instant replay will be the best part of all!

WORD GAMES

Word games are the easiest because you need no materials at all. Here are some you can try. Sometimes you may have to simplify the rules so the youngest players can join in too.

If I Were a Purple Cow

Someone starts a sentence, letting each of the others make up a silly ending.

EXAMPLE:

"If I were a purple cow, I would love to eat _____."
"If I were a TV star, I would change my name to _____."
"If I were a teacher, I would allow more time for the class to _____."

Whose line got the most laughs?

Peanut Butter and Jelly

Take turns thinking of combinations of words that go together. Say the first word in the series and let the others fill in the blanks:

cream and _____
shoes and _____

If I were a purple cow I would love to eat...

Pickles!

Blecch!

107

(continued on next page)

Or say the first two words:

red, white, and _____
get ready, get set, _____
bacon, lettuce, and _____
yesterday, today, and _____

Or group words that go together in *categories:*

Denver, Miami, and _____ (cities)
beans, carrots, and _____ (vegetables)
Ford, Chevrolet, and _____ (cars)

Poison

Choose a word that's used a lot, like "I," "said," or "when," and call it "poison." Every time someone uses that word, he gets a penalty point. See who has the *fewest* points in a 10-minute period.

"I bet the next car will be from Arizona."

"I bet it won't."

I Bet

This is the only word game that requires any materials. Just bring along some pennies, bottle caps, or poker chips to use for betting. Give everyone five or six pennies, or whatever you're using, so that one by one each player can make a wager. "I bet the next car will be _____." (Mention color, type, number of passengers, a two-door or four-door model, the state on the license plate, and so forth.) Whoever wants to bet against you can but must give you a penny if he's wrong. If *you* are wrong, you lose and must pay a penny to everyone who bet against you. The player with the most pennies at the end of a given time or mile limit is the winner.

Alphabet Games

There are also many word games that are built on letters of the alphabet.

ALPHABET NAMES

Choose a letter and take turns calling out a boy's or girl's name that begins with that letter. The game continues until everyone runs out of ideas. Example: Alice, Annabelle, Andy. When you can't think of any more A's, start with a new letter, like E: Ellen, Ethel, Edward. You'll be the winner if you can think up unusual names, like Archibald or Englebert, and be the last one to say a name.

I ADORE MY PET GORILLA

"I adore my pet gorilla with an A because she is _____." Take turns completing this sentence, adding words from A to Z. The first player using the letter A could say, "I adore my pet gorilla with an A because she is arty" (or athletic). The next might say, "I adore my pet gorilla with a B because she's bouncy," or batty, or whatever pops into your mind. The third player uses the letter C (cute, clumsy, corny). Older children can test their memories by repeating each word in alphabetical order. "I adore my pet gorilla because she is *athletic*, *bouncy*, and *clumsy*." This could become a real tongue twister.

Another Way: For each round, change the word "adore" to follow the alphabet too: I *bought* my pet gorilla with a B because _____." "I *cuddle* my pet gorilla with a C _____."

ALCATRAZ TO ZANZIBAR

Also going from A to Z, try to name, from memory, cities, states, countries, mountains, oceans, rivers, or lakes. Alabama, Billings, China . . .

A-TO-Z LICENSE PLATES

Look out the window and help each other find all the letters of the alphabet, in order. Watch the road signs and the license plates of passing cars as you drive along.

THE HOME STRETCH

Here is a "wordless" game that will no doubt be started by the driver!

Break the Silence

At a signal, everyone tries to remain quiet for as long as possible. Whoever makes a noise is out and will then try to make the others talk. The one who keeps silent the longest wins.

Singing in the Car

Singing passes the hours quickly. When you tire of your favorites, make up your own travel songs to go with familiar tunes. Here is an example, to the tune of "Frère Jacques":

"We are driving, we are driving,
To the beach, to the beach . . ."

Other ways: Hum the beginning of a song and see who can finish it; or choose a category like the sun or the moon and see how many songs you can sing about it: "You Are My Sunshine" and "Paper Moon," for example. More ideas for categories found in songs are: names of states, cities, girls and boys, and so forth: "Oklahoma," "London Bridge," "Michael, Row the Boat Ashore."

Backseat Exercises

Did you know that there are exercises that everyone can do, even though you're cramped together in the back seat?* Try *stretching* each part of your body as far as you can, counting as you go. *Example:* first extend your right leg, chanting, "Leg 2-3-4, stretch 2-3-4"; then your left leg, repeating the chant; then both legs. Next stretch your neck: "neck 2-3-4, stretch 2-3-4." Stretch your arms, keeping the rhythm going. Turn on the radio and try these "sit-down" movements: hunch your shoulders one at a time, roll your knees, or shift your weight from side to side.

Pretend you are a turtle disappearing into its shell by pulling in your arms, legs, and head as tightly as you can: "close 2-3-4." Then slowly open up again: "open 2-3-4."

You don't really have to move at all — just squeezing your muscles tight is good exercise. Fold your arms and press them against your body; hold in your tummy; touch your elbows, clench your fists; tighten your lips. Don't forget to wiggle your ears!

*If you have a car full of people, do these exercises one person at a time.

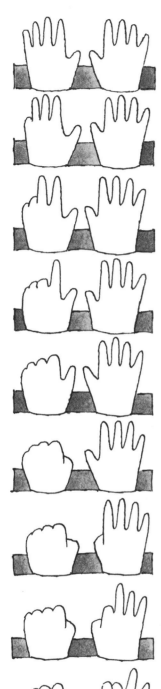

Exercise your fingers, too. Here is a finger game to get you started:

Ten in the Bed

Start with all 10 fingers extended, and each time you say "one fell out," drop a finger until there are none left. Every time you come to the phrase "roll over," make a rolling motion with your hands and arms.

There were ten in the bed
And the little one said,
"Roll over, roll over."
So they all rolled over
And one fell out.

There were nine in the bed
And the little one said,
"Roll over, roll over," etc.

When you come to "There was *one* in the bed," substitute your own name for "the little one," ending the verse with "And Lisa said, 'Good Night!'"

STOP FOR THE NIGHT

You can continue to enjoy your puppets, Flannel Board, and other car toys when you stop for the night. It's also a good time to listen to your recordings and to use some of the postcards collected along the way to make a Travelog or puzzle.

Double Puzzles

YOU NEED: picture postcards
glue
scissors
envelope

YOU DO:

1. Glue *two* postcards together back to back; then, when the glue is dry, cut them into pieces to make a *pair of puzzles*.
2. Put the pieces into an envelope so they won't get lost.

Travelog

1. Paste your postcards on sheets of construction paper to keep a daily log of your travels.
2. Add paper napkins, matchbook covers, admission stubs, museum guides, or whatever mementos you've collected.
3. Date each page and write a sentence or two, if you have time.

Don't forget to mail a few postcards to your friends at home, too!

GUIDE TO LEARNING CONCEPTS FOUND IN *TRAVELING*

In this chapter a majority of the activities sharpen a child's observation and listening skills while traveling along. By watching the "world out the window" or finding creative ways to enjoy the car radio and tape recorder, a child can depend on his eyes and ears to pass the hours constructively.

ACTIVITIES (Page)	MOVEMENT/MOTOR COORDINATION large	small	CREATIVITY/MAKING THINGS	LANGUAGE DEVELOPMENT/COMMUNICATION oral	written	READING AND MATH SKILL-BUILDING	PROBLEM-SOLVING/DISCOVERY	IMAGINATIVE PLAY/SELF-EXPRESSION
Take-Along Snacks (94)		X						
Trip Tape (95)		X	X	X		X	X	
Pretend Driving (96)	X	X	X	X				X
Magic Peepers (97)		X	X			X		X
Purple Cow Bingo (98)		X	X	X		X	X	
Keep-Busy Box (99)		X				X	X	X
Flannel Board (100)		X	X	X		X		X
Box-Lid Puppet Theater (100)		X	X	X			X	X
Finger Puppets (101); Pop-up Puppets (102)		X	X	X				
Story Fill-ins (103)				X		X		X
Traveling Tales (104)		X		X			X	X
What's Next? (105)				X				X
Radio Word Game (105)				X		X		
Name the Tune (105)				X			X	
Invent a Game (106)				X			X	X
If I Were a Purple Cow (107)				X			X	X
Peanut Butter and Jelly (107)				X		X	X	
Poison (108)				X				
I Bet (108)				X		X		
Alphabet Names (109)				X		X		
I Adore My Pet Gorilla (109)				X		X		X
Alcatraz to Zanzibar (109)				X		X		
A-to-Z License Plates (109)				X		X		
Break the Silence (110)				X				
Singing in the Car (110)				X			X	X
Backseat Exercises (111)	X	X		X		X		X
"Ten in the Bed" (112)	X	X		X		X		X
Double Puzzles (113)			X		X			
Travelog (113)		X	X	X		X		

PURPLE COW TO THE RESCUE . . .
When You're Moving

Moving, whether it's to a city far away or just to another street in your own town, means many changes, but your move can become an adventure! The key is planning ahead and involving the whole family in the project.

It's

- talking about what needs to be done
- investigating what's yet to come
- saving "reminders" from your old home; making a floor plan of the new one
- looking forward to new friends
- discovering as much as you can about your new neighborhood so its "newness" will soon wear off
- planning your clothes to fit the weather — will you be wearing a bathing suit or building a snowman on your *next* birthday?

Even if *you* aren't moving, you can use many of these ideas to help welcome or say good-bye to someone who is.

PLANNING AHEAD

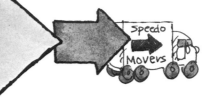

Moving Along

Look at a map and *trace the route* you'll be taking to drive to your new home, or the one that the moving van will probably use to deliver your toys and clothes to you!

YOU NEED:

cardboard, a box lid, or heavy paper
crayons or felt-tip markers
U.S., state, or local map
glue
construction paper
scissors
buttons, bottle caps, egg-carton sections, or
    tiny boxes for markers
dice

YOU DO:

1. Draw or glue the map onto the cardboard, marking north, south, east, and west so you can see which direction you'll be traveling.
2. Locate both your old and new homes and draw pictures of each to mark your start and finish.
3. Next, draw a double line showing the route between the two houses and mark off squares between the lines.
4. Circle the big cities, towns, and interesting sights along the way. Look for rivers and national forests, bridges and famous buildings.
5. Make markers (a different color or object for each player) to look like a car, train, plane, bus, or boat. Cut them out of construction paper and glue them onto the bottle caps or buttons. You might even build a multicolored fleet of moving vans by adding wheels, windows, and doors to the egg cups or boxes.

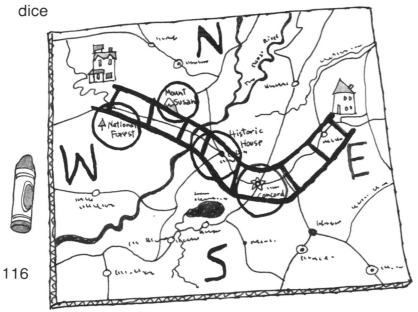

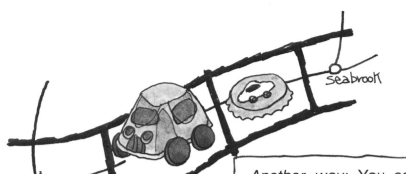

6. Take turns throwing the dice and moving that number of squares along the route.
7. The first player to arrive at the new house is the winner.

Another way: You can *measure* the distance between the two houses and let the squares stand for a set number of miles or kilometers. You might need a math whiz to help with this!

Home Plate

Play another board game to learn more about the new area where you'll be living. Since your parents have probably already visited your new hometown, they can tell you some things you can expect to see and do; or they could write to the local Chamber of Commerce or State Tourist Bureau for maps, brochures, and pictures that you can use.

YOU NEED:

a paper plate
crayons or markers
dice
buttons or bottle caps (for markers)

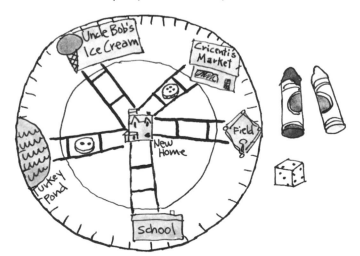

YOU DO:

1. Using a paper plate for your game board, put your "new home" as the starting place in the center and mark off separate routes with the same number of squares leading to each local spot (the ballpark, school, ice-cream parlor, supermarket, gas station, lake, or swimming pool).
2. Each player chooses a place to visit and, in turn, throws the dice, trying to be the first to get there and back home again.
3. Your final throw must equal the *exact* number needed to land on home, or else you cannot move at all.

117

REMINDERS

You'll probably want to take along a few souvenirs to remind you of your old home and friends. A special box of your favorite things, a memory poster, an autographed stuffed animal, or picture pendants are all good keepsakes.

Remember-Me Pictures

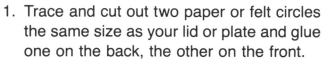

YOU NEED:

metal or plastic jar lids, paper plates, or pie tins
construction paper or felt scraps
scissors
glue
photos or pictures
yarn, braid, or rickrack

YOU DO:

1. Trace and cut out two paper or felt circles the same size as your lid or plate and glue one on the back, the other on the front.
2. Draw a picture of someone you'd like to remember, or cut out a small photo; then glue it inside the lid or plate.
3. Now add some trim around the edges.
4. To make a memory necklace, poke a hole at the top of the lid with a hammer and nail and push ribbon or yarn through for hanging.

You might make lid pictures of several friends and relatives. Attach the pictures to a hanger or dowel for a mobile; glue them onto a wide ribbon for a wall hanging; or display them on a cardboard stand covered with felt or brightly colored fabric. You can also use a ring from a plastic six-pack holder to "frame" your picture or use the entire holder for a collection of six pictures.

Memory Poster

YOU NEED:

"bits of this and that"
cardboard, a large box lid, or an old window
   shade
glue
paintbrush

AFTER GLUING:

GLUE water

PAINT OVER THE
REMINDERS WITH
A THIN COAT OF
GLUE AND WATER
TO MAKE IT
SHINY.

YOU DO:

1. Gather up some reminders of your old home and friends, like a ball-game stub, greeting card or party invitation from someone "special," a pressed flower or leaf from your yard, or a leftover swatch of fabric or wallpaper from your room.
2. Have your friends give you pictures of themselves and their pets, and recipe cards of special foods that you have enjoyed eating at their homes. Maybe they'd like to write their signatures on a card for you too.
3. Glue all the reminders onto the cardboard or window shade in a free-form design. Then paint over it with a thin coat of white glue mixed with a little water; this will dry clear and leave a shiny finish.

Your Memory Poster will be all ready to hang on the wall of your new bedroom.

Autograph Hound

YOU NEED:

two pieces of solid-colored cloth or an
   old pillowcase
common (straight) pins
a pencil
scissors
a needle

thread
stuffing (cut-up hose, rags, old socks, or foam
   padding)
buttons
a ball-point pen

YOU DO:

1. Carefully pin the two pieces of cloth together with the *wrong* sides facing out.
2. Draw the outline of an animal on the cloth and then draw a second outline inside it, about one inch away. Use a simple shape like a dog, pig, or penguin.
3. Now carefully cut around the *outside* line.
4. Thread the needle with a long piece of thread, double it, and knot the end. Sew along the *inside* line, using the basic running stitch, and leave an opening for stuffing. (See diagram.)
5. Turn the material back to the right side, and push the stuffing through the opening, packing it in tightly. Be sure you have filled all of the corners before sewing up the hole.
6. Then sew or glue on buttons for the eyes.
7. Hang a ball-point pen around the neck of the autograph hound with a ribbon and ask all your friends to sign their names on it.

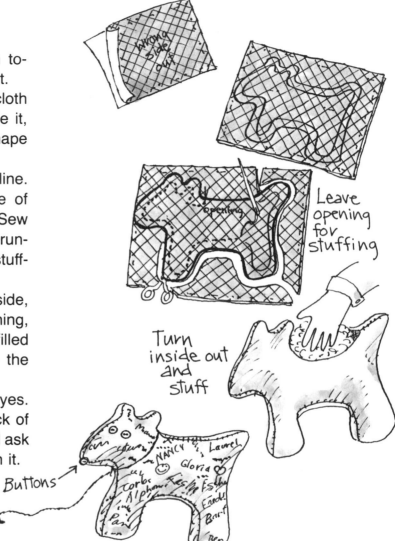

Leave opening for stuffing

Turn inside out and stuff

Buttons →

Keeping in Touch

Fill out an address book so that you can write letters, postcards, and greeting cards to your friends and relatives "back home." You can make your own address book using lined file cards or construction paper; punch a hole in two corners and tie with yarn or ribbon. You could also file the cards in a decorated box.

It's fun to make your own stationery too. Decorate plain postcards or notepaper, using crayons, felt-tip markers, peel-off stickers, or your clay stamper (see page 83).

Since you'll want to get lots of letters when you first arrive, ask for some change-of-address cards at the post office. Have your parents write out some extra ones for you to deliver to your friends before you leave. Then you can look forward to a full mailbox at your new home. To be doubly sure that there's something waiting for you, send a welcome letter to yourself. How many days ahead will you have to mail your letter so it will get there before *you* do?

The everyday sounds all around you can be recorded as still another reminder of home. Most of these noises are so familiar that you probably don't even notice them.

Sounds of Home

Floors and doors that creak and squeak
A teapot that whistles
A faucet dripping, a radiator hissing
A shutter banging in the wind
Sounds of home I often hear
But never really hear at all.

Go from room to room, close your eyes, and listen carefully to all of the noises. Choose the ones you'd like to "keep" and put the tape recorder up close to catch each sound.

There are a lot of familiar outdoor noises for you to record, too: the songs of the local birds feeding on your windowsill, the whistle of a nearby train, neighbors calling their children in for dinner, a garbage can clanking, traffic on the street. Do you think you will hear the same sounds in your new neighborhood? After the move you can listen to your recording and compare the sounds.

You might want to include "talking labels" or little stories to keep track of each sound. ("This is Pancho, the dog next door, waking us up early each morning.") Luckily *your* dog's bark or cat's meow will probably go along with you.

You'll want to remember the sounds of your friends' voices too. Before you pack up, ask them to record a special good-bye message. Long after, when you've almost forgotten what everything looks like, you'll still have reminders each time you play back your tapes.

see you next summer!

Take-Along Room

How about designing a mini-bedroom that you can take with you? Decorate a box to look like *your old room;* later you can change it to fit your new one.

1. Make miniature copies of your furniture from tiny boxes, egg-carton cups, Popsicle sticks, or whatever you have around. Cloth scraps are useful for curtains, bedspreads, towels, and tablecloths.

2. Place your bed, dresser, bookcases, and other furniture where they are now.

3. Next you'll want to rearrange them to fit your new room. Find out the basic shape of the room and where the doors and windows are located. Close your eyes and try to picture how you would want your new room to look. Where will your bed be? Your toy shelves or dresser? Will there be anything new, like a desk or a bulletin board? Be sure to leave a space for it.

4. Mark the spot where you've decided to put each thing so you can help the movers when they carry in your real furniture.

5. Later you could cover the walls and floors of your Take-Along Room with leftover paint, wallpaper, and carpet scraps from the new house.

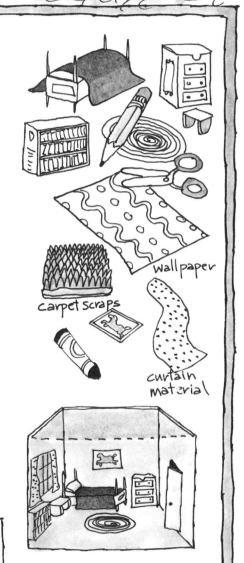

wallpaper

carpet scraps

curtain material

Another way: You could use a large cardboard box, adding movable dividers that you've made by notching pieces of cardboard. Then you can change the arrangement of the rooms to look like your old house and new one too.

MOVING TIPS

Moving

Open the suitcase — I'm ready to pack;
In goes my train set
In goes my track.
In go my books and all of my toys
I'm off to meet some new girls and boys.

Open the suitcase — now I am there;
Out comes my Snoopy
Out comes my bear
Out come my books and all of my toys
I'm ready to meet the new girls and boys!

Packing Tips

1. It's tempting to get rid of things to lighten the load, but hold on to those items that you'd really miss. A few extra pounds won't matter, and you can always give them up later.
2. Make the move easier by going around the house with your parents "tagging" the furniture (perhaps in different colors) to show where it will be placed in your new home.
3. Mark the boxes that go into *your* room with your own trademark: a picture, your name or initials, or a printed symbol made with your clay stamper (p. 83).

(continued on next page)

4. Set aside the larger things that you will want handy when you arrive at your new home. Be sure they are the *last* to go into the van so they'll be the *first* to come out. Your trusty bicycle will be ready for your first ride down your new block. Familiar things like bath toys will be especially welcome, since they'll make everyday routines seem more like home.

5. Pack up a special *arrival kit* for some quick home projects to keep you busy when the movers are settling you in your new home. Put in a roll of shelf paper or an old window shade for a mural (p. 119), a vinyl tablecloth for a table setting (p. 50), and a few magazines for any number of easy projects you can do before everything else is unpacked. Be sure that this kit goes in the back of the van too.

Take-Along Tips

1. Before the moving van is packed, rescue a few of your personal items like a toothbrush, comb, favorite blanket, and change of clothes, and pack them in an overnight case.

2. Take along a shopping bag or treasure box with your name or trademark on it to hold crayons, paper, a deck of cards, and toys and games that are small enough to carry with you. (For more take-along ideas, look at "Traveling," pages 93 to 114, where you'll find Magic Peepers, Keep-Busy Box, Flannel Board, Box-Lid Theater, Finger Puppets, Pop-up Puppets, and many more.)

3. Don't forget to bring your stuffed animal and a favorite book for a bedtime story. They will be old friends the first night in your new home.

Arrival Tips for Parents

1. If you're moving for the first time to a house with stairs, bring along a safety gate and pack it near the back of the truck so it can be put to immediate use for toddlers.
2. It's not the best time to change a child to a new bed. Try to do this long before the move or wait until later after the adjustment to moving has been made.
3. Don't forget a night light for those first few weeks in unfamiliar surroundings.

Home at Last

Now that you're finally home, pull out your "arrival kit" and start some projects. First of all, let everyone know you've moved in! Just write your name and house number on a paper plate or the flap of a packing box, tape or glue it to a ruler or stick, and poke it into the ground right in front of your new house.

Make another special sign with great big letters to announce who lives in your room. (See page 25 for ideas.)

GETTING ACQUAINTED

Be an Explorer

After the empty moving truck has left and before you start unpacking, why not take a break and explore your new neighborhood? The best place to start is right on your own block. Pretend you are wearing giant magnifying glasses so you can take a close-up look at all the new things around you.

An *alphabet hunt* will give you special things to look for and make you a better explorer! Before you start out, put together a list of things that are in most neighborhoods.

A — apartment buildings
B — basketball hoop, brick wall
C — car, curtains
D — driveway, door knocker

Check off each one that you find and add new things as you spot them.

P — picket fence
W — window box

Did you meet any pets along the way? If you saw a wagon or tricycle outside a house, these are "clues" that there are some children living inside!

126

Picture Your Rooms

To get to know the layout of your new house, make cards for the rooms and arrange them in a floor plan.

YOU NEED: cardboard
scissors
crayons
magazine or newspaper pictures
glue

YOU DO:

1. Take a walk inside your house or apartment. Count the number of rooms and name each one.
2. Cut out cardboard squares, one for each room.
3. Then go back and look at the rooms again. On each square card, draw or paste a picture of something that goes in the room (a stove for the kitchen, a couch for the living room, a dresser for the bedroom, and so forth).
4. Now arrange the cards to look like your house, with each room in its proper place.
5. Shuffle the cards and make a game of putting the house back in order!

As you get older: Notice the sizes and shapes of the rooms and cut your cardboard to match (L-shaped living room; long rectangular hall; small, square bathroom). If you'd like to make the rooms to scale, measure each one in feet and then draw it in inches, letting one inch equal one foot. Then you can fit all the rooms together like a giant puzzle.

NEW FRIENDS

It takes time to know the people in your new neighborhood. If the moving van doesn't bring out some curious onlookers, why not be brave and make the *first* move yourself? Here are some "icebreakers" to help your family meet the new neighbors.

A New-Neighbor Get-Together

1. Have your parents invite one or two families over for a short visit, maybe just an hour, for a treat and a game or two.
2. Ask the children to bring a favorite toy, book, or family picture to share.
3. Have all the guests make a name tag as they arrive. You'll need construction paper, scissors, and crayons. (Use some of the ideas on page 25.)

128

Sandwich Swap

One way to get acquainted is to have a picnic-style party. For lunch, ask everyone to bring a favorite sandwich, cut in quarters to *trade* with three new friends.

SANDWICH IDEAS:

SUBMARINES

Cut a long French roll in half lengthwise and spread with mayonnaise or mustard. Then pile on as many kinds of sliced luncheon meats and cheeses as you want, adding tomatoes, onions, pickles, lettuce, and so forth. Cut into four parts for your swap.

SAILBOATS

Make a sandwich with three pieces of bread instead of two. Use two kinds of fillings that will go together, such as peanut butter and jelly, tuna and egg salad, ham and swiss cheese, cream cheese and banana slices, and so forth. Cut your sandwich into four triangles and stand each one up on end for a sail. Serve it on a hard-boiled egg half, "floating" on a leaf of lettuce.

ZOO SANDWICHES

Cut your bread into animal shapes with cookie cutters (or cut around simple cardboard patterns). Use whatever fillings you'd like and then stand your "animals" up on a paper plate. (Three slices of bread will work better than two.)

For added fun, serve your zoo animals in cages made from a berry basket or an open box standing on its side, with drinking-straw "bars" taped to the front. Be sure to make four sandwiches so you'll have enough to trade.

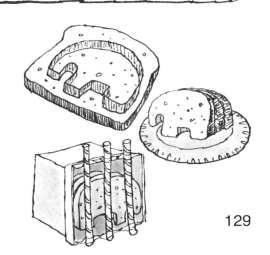

Drop-in Cookies

You may just want to have "afternoon tea" with lemonade and cookies. Here's a way to make three different kinds of cookies out of just *one* dough. Start with this basic recipe for sugar-cookie dough; roll and cut it into different shapes (like your new state — just follow a cardboard pattern), or add ingredients such as peanut butter or chocolate chips.

BASIC DOUGH (makes two batches, or approximately 80 cookies)

YOU NEED:

2 eggs
⅔ cup shortening
⅔ cup butter or margarine, softened
1½ cups sugar
3½ cups all-purpose flour
2 teaspoons baking powder
1 teaspoon salt
2 teaspoons vanilla

YOU DO:

1. Beat eggs and add the rest of the ingredients in the order given.
2. Mix on low speed ½ minute, then blend well on medium speed.
3. Form into 2 balls with your hands (add 1 tablespoon of cream to each ball if it does not stick together). Each ball makes about 40 cookies.

PEANUT-BUTTER-AND-JAM COOKIES

1. To half of the basic dough, add ⅔ cup of peanut butter.
2. Roll the dough between your hands into little balls, place on an ungreased baking sheet, and flatten with a fork.
3. Bake at 375° about 12 minutes (don't let them get too hard).
4. When cool, make "sandwiches" by spreading jam between two cookies.

CHOCOLATE OR BUTTERSCOTCH SQUARES

1. To half of the basic cookie dough, mix in one 6-ounce package of chocolate chips or butterscotch pieces and ½ cup of chopped nuts.
2. Press dough into ungreased 13×9×2 pan and bake at 375° for 20–25 minutes.
3. Cut into squares while warm.

130

New-Neighbor Games

Here are some games to help you and your new neighbors get better acquainted:

TRADE-A-NAME

YOU NEED:

construction paper (different color for each player)
scissors
crayon or felt-tip marker
paste, glue, or stapler

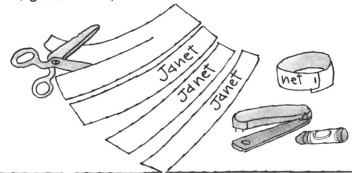

YOU DO:

1. Cut your construction paper into several long strips and write your name on each one.
2. Trade one of your strips with each of the other players.
3. Put together a multicolored paper chain of all the names to wear around your wrist or neck. (Plastic six-pack holders could also be cut apart, labeled with a felt-tip pen, and tied together with yarn or ribbon.) Watch the chain grow as you trade with each new friend.

WHO HAS?

Make up a list of questions for the group to answer. Who has the widest smile? Who has the most pets? This game will help you to get to know each other quickly.

Who has the longest name? (Christopher)
Who was born the farthest away (Clarinha)
Who has the most freckles? (Peter)
Who's wearing the most colors? (Roger)

Another way: Make a different kind of list to find out what everyone likes and dislikes: favorite and least favorite color, book, dessert or snack food, TV program, comic strip. Do your new friends like the same things as you? Tally up the answers to find out how each person is alike and different.

This can be a team game when there is a large group.

PAPER CHASE

Here's another team game with a list of questions that will help you get to know your *new hometown.*

1. Before the party, ask each neighbor to bring a copy of yesterday's newspaper (or collect some back issues, all the same date, from a news dealer — sometimes they even give those away free!)
2. Give each team (or player, if the group is small) an identical newspaper and a copy of the list of questions to answer.
3. Some examples to hunt for:

   What time did the sun rise?
   What were the high and low temperatures?
   Which store has a sale?
   Did the local team win or lose?
   What famous person had her picture in the paper?

4. Write in the answers and put down the page numbers where you found them.
5. Share your answers and see how many things you've learned about your new city.

I'M HOME NOW (a packing-box game)

YOU NEED:

packing boxes (1 for each player, so don't throw them all away!)
crayons or felt-tip markers
construction paper or cardboard
scissors
piano, radio, record player, or whistle (if music is not readily available)

YOU DO:

1. Each player writes his name and address on a packing box and decorates it to look like his *own* house.
2. Arrange the "houses" on the floor to match their order on the block.

3. To begin the game, players move around the room to music until the leader (an adult or older child) turns it off. Then everyone scrambles to his *own* home and either stoops behind it or gets inside (if he fits!), quickly calling out, "I'm home now."

4. As the game moves on, make it more challenging by allowing the players to stop at *any* house. Now when the music stops, the leader calls, "Where's John?" John then pops out and answers, "I'm at Alexis's house."

You'll quickly learn where your neighbors live with this game!

Another game that you and your new friends will enjoy playing is Home Plate, the board game about your new town (p. 117).

WINDOW-SHADE MURAL

Here's a party activity that will brighten the bare walls of your new house! All you need is an old window shade, either one you've brought along or one that was left behind.

Spread newspapers on the floor, unroll the shade in the middle of them, and pass out the crayons and markers. In a short time you'll have a group mural with everyone taking a part in decorating the house. Have each artist sign his name on the mural so you'll always remember who came to your first party in your new neighborhood.

Just before the party is over, collect all the clean or unused leftovers — paper plates, cups, straws, boxes — and put together a Junk Sculpture (see page 88). This will be a nice way to wrap up the party and you'll end up with another original decoration for your new room.

Packing-Box Pretending

Once you've settled in, you'll be ready to tackle a bigger project. Large packing boxes have all sorts of possibilities, so be sure to save one. You and your new friends can turn it into a make-believe grocery store, a fort, a space ship, fire station, schoolhouse, ticket or telephone booth, or just a secret hideaway.

YOU NEED: a large cardboard packing box
knife (Be sure an adult does the cutting.)
scissors
crepe paper
paints, crayons, or felt-tip markers
construction paper
glue

YOU DO:
1. First decide together what you'd like your box to be.
2. Then ask an adult to cut a door in one of the sides so you can get in and out.
3. Now decorate the box to fit your theme. Here are some ideas:

PUPPET THEATER

Cut a large square opening in the top half of one side for the stage. For a curtain that can be taken in or out, glue colorful crepe-paper streamers onto a cardboard hanger tube; hang the curtain across two hooks or nails placed on either side of the stage.

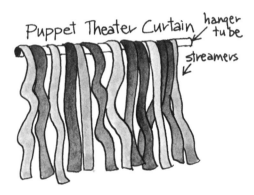

Another way: Decorate an old window shade and use it as a curtain or backdrop.

SPACESHIP

Cut a circle in the center of one side and cover the box with foil. Glue on rocket engines made of cardboard tubes, foil pie pans, jar lids, and anything else you can find around the house that's bright and shiny. On the inside, you could draw or glue on an instrument panel.

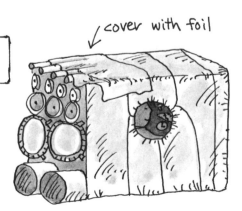

SWEET SHOP

Cut out a large window opening in the box, leaving the top side attached for a striped awning or the bottom for a counter. On the outside of the shop, draw shelves with jars, and glue on wrapped candy to "fill" them.

You'll have four times as much fun with just one box by making *each* side different. Then you can be an astronaut, storekeeper, or puppeteer by just turning the box around.

Welcome Wagon

Now *you're* the "old-timer" in the neighborhood. But do you remember how you felt when you first arrived? When the next moving van pulls into your block, maybe you'll use some of the ideas in this chapter to say hello to a new family. If you know ahead of time that new neighbors are moving in, you might post a welcome sign, hang a basket of wildflowers on their door, invite them to a "sandwich swap," or gather a group together to set up a Welcome Wagon.

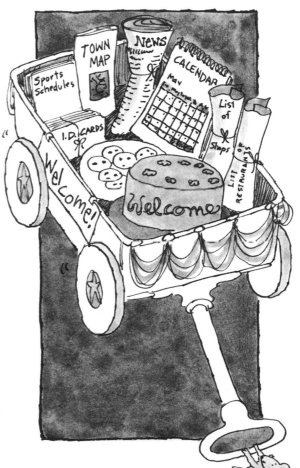

1. Fill a wagon with all kinds of information about your neighborhood: a local newspaper and map; a calendar of special events in your town, such as a county fair or circus; a schedule of baseball, basketball, or football games; or lists of shops and restaurants.
2. For a surprise gift, add a home-baked cake or some cookies, or anything else a newcomer might like.
3. Have everyone make an ID card with name, age, address, and class in school to include in the wagon. You can make an ID card for each of your pets too.

GUIDE TO LEARNING CONCEPTS FOUND IN
MOVING

Creative activities for helping a child make the move to a new home can do more than just acquaint him with his surroundings. The craft projects and games in this chapter give opportunities for developing language, reading, and math skills, while dealing with the many changes that go along with moving.

ACTIVITIES (Page)	MOVEMENT/ MOTOR COORDINATION large/small	CREATIVITY/ MAKING THINGS	LANGUAGE DEVELOPMENT COMMUNICATION oral/written	READING AND MATH SKILL-BUILDING	PROBLEM-SOLVING/ DISCOVERY	IMAGINATIVE PLAY/ SELF-EXPRESSION
Moving Along (116)	X	X	X	X	X	
Home Plate (117)	X	X		X	X	
Remember-Me Pictures (118)	X	X				
Memory Poster (119)	X	X				
Autograph Hound (119)	X	X		X		
Keeping in Touch (120)	X	X	X	X		
"Sounds of Home" (121)			X	X	X	
Take-Along Room (122)	X	X		X	X	
"Moving" (123)			X			X
Home at Last (125)	X	X		X		
Be an Explorer (126)	X X		X	X	X	X
Picture Your Rooms (127)	X		X	X	X	
Sandwich Swap (129); Drop-in Cookies (130)	X	X		X		
Trade-a-Name (131)	X	X	X			
Who Has? (131)			X	X	X	
Paper Chase (132)	X		X	X	X	
I'm Home Now (132)	X X	X	X	X	X	X
Window-Shade Mural (133)	X	X				
Packing-Box Pretending (134)	X X	X				X
Welcome Wagon (135)			X		X	X

PURPLE COW TO THE RESCUE . . .
When You're Winding Down

After a busy morning, or any hour of the day when you need to take a break, these quiet-time activities will help you to unwind. Nighttime is a special time for parents and children to relax together after a full day of work and play.

It's

- sharing a success or a worry
- indoor fun with a tape recorder
- a project with yesterday's newspaper
- a quiet game, a pillow surprise
- catching a first glimpse of "star light, star bright"
    - and "just one more bedtime story . . . please."

The ideas in this chapter for winding down at nighttime or naptime can help you at other times, too. Use them when you're sick in bed or stuck inside on a rainy or snowy day.

cow slippers

SETTLING DOWN

Powwow

Find a quiet moment at home or at school and call a powwow to talk about what happened that day. Who has a funny story to tell or something new to share? A powwow is also a good time to give someone a compliment or to tell what's "bugging" you on a day when things don't seem to go right.

Pass the Bug Box

YOU NEED:

2 egg cartons
scissors
crayons or felt-tip markers
pipe cleaners

YOU DO:

1. Give every member of the class or family an egg-carton cup to make his own bug.
2. Draw on spots and add pipe-cleaner "feelers" and legs. Then each person writes his name on his bug.
3. Sit in a circle and pass around a bug box (a decorated egg or oatmeal carton).
4. When you feel like telling what's "bugging" you, put your bug into the box and it's *your* turn to talk.

Another way: This could also be called a *buzz session!* Change the bug box to a beehive (an upside-down margarine tub with its lid on and a "door" cut into the side). Make the bees out of cotton balls, yarn pompoms, or peanut shells.

Add a Character

There are many ways to express your feelings when something is bothering you. One way is to make up your own *soap opera* and talk out some problems, such as having to do chores, and daily routines that aren't much fun, or settling a disagreement with a friend or family member. How would you solve problems like these through a soap opera?

It's time for bed and your favorite TV program is just starting.

Great-aunt Tillie is coming to visit for a month, and she's staying in *your* room.

Mom says, "I need everyone to pitch in and help get the Thanksgiving dinner together."

"Why do I have to drag Nancy along with me and my friends? She's too young."

"Do I really have to stay in from recess to finish the test?"

1. Choose a theme for your soap opera and talk about how you would act it out.
2. Then decide who will play each role.
3. Begin by having each character walk on "stage" and make up a few lines to set the scene. The other characters appear when it's their turn to take part in the story.
4. There's no need for a script, props, or scenery. The important thing is for each person to express real feelings in real situations.

Good Feelings

Praise makes us all feel good, so use your Powwow to share positive thoughts and feelings.

1. Sit down and talk about the things you like about other people: "smiles a lot," "shares his sandwich," "plays fair."
2. Give everyone a pencil and a set of cards (or slips of paper).
3. Write down the name of each person in the group on your set of cards. Then turn each card over and write something nice about that person — a quality of his or hers that you like. (If you can't write yet, tell your ideas to someone who can.)
4. Collect the cards and sort them, giving each person his own stack of "good feelings."
5. Now take turns reading your cards aloud. Later you could make a mobile, scrapbook, or collage by gluing the cards onto a colorful cut-out in the shape of something you like, such as a record, an apple, a heart. Add a picture of yourself to complete your "good feelings" collage or mobile.

Choose a Chore

Cleanup time can be more fun if you make a game out of it.

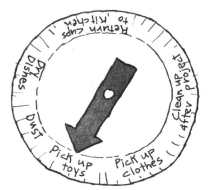

1. Think of all of the "end-of-the-day" chores that need doing; then write them down on a pad of paper or on the chalkboard:

SCHOOL LIST
- Put books back on the shelves
- Erase the chalkboard
- Stack up the blocks

HOME LIST
- Pick up toys or clothes
- Clean up after a project
- Return stray cups to the Kitchen

2. Write all of the chores around the edge of a paper plate, attach a cardboard arrow with a brad at the center, and *spin* to find your cleanup job.

TALKING TIME

Do you have a tape recorder, slide projector, or record player? These can give you hours of "quiet time" talking activities.

Tape a Tale

During the day, make some recordings — a favorite story, something funny that happened to you, a song, or a silly poem — then play the tape back at bedtime. If you come up with a really good tape, you may decide to save it to replay on a rainy day or on a long car trip, or even mail it to Grandma as a "talking letter."

The following activities can be enjoyed with or without a tape recorder; if you do have one, the playback will make you sound like you're a radio star.

Cat Chat

Make believe you are having a chat with a real or imaginary animal. What kind of questions would you ask? Can you play both parts yourself by inventing an animal voice?

Sixty Seconds

Talk for one minute about any subject you choose. Here are some ideas:

"What I would put in the biggest Dagwood sandwich in the world."

"How I'd dress if I were invited to Cinderella's ball."

"Sometimes my dog (cat) acts like a person."

Do Your Own Radio Show

Tell a story such as "Hansel and Gretel," disguising your voice to fit each character. For sound effects, crumple up a sheet of paper to imitate the crackling leaves in the forest; whistle when it's time for the birds to chirp; and tap with your knuckles when Hansel and Gretel knock on the door of the cottage. Background music will heighten the suspense of the story.

You could also make radio stars out of comic-strip characters by acting out scenes from your favorite Sunday funnies. What kind of voice would you give Marmaduke or Garfield?

Ad-libs

Have you ever made up a TV commercial? It's fun — especially if you invent your own products to advertise:

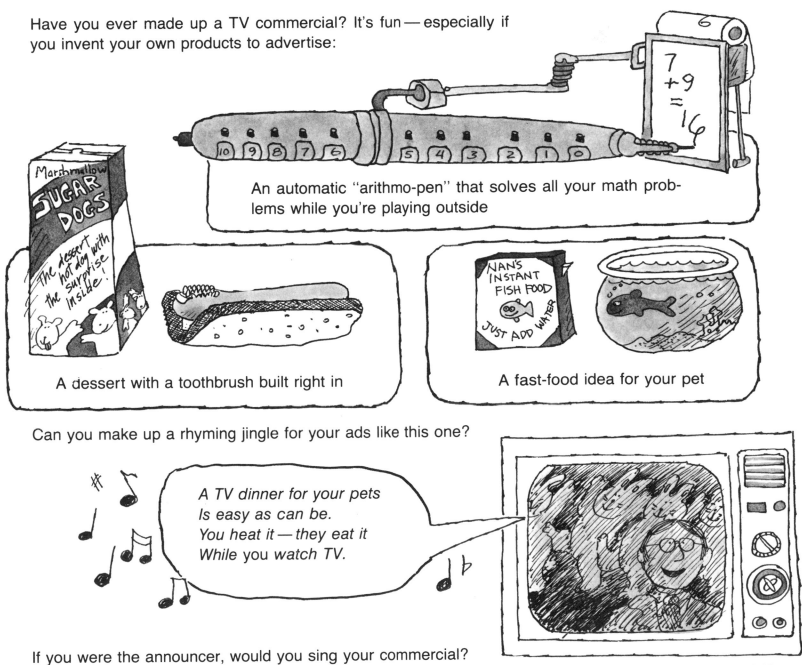

An automatic "arithmo-pen" that solves all your math problems while you're playing outside

A dessert with a toothbrush built right in

A fast-food idea for your pet

Can you make up a rhyming jingle for your ads like this one?

*A TV dinner for your pets
Is easy as can be.
You heat it — they eat it
While you watch TV.*

If you were the announcer, would you sing your commercial?

143

QUIET GAMES

sshhh!! quiet as a mouse...

When you're winding down, sometimes you're in the mood for talking, and at other times, you may feel like playing some quiet games that you've made yourself.

Popsicle-Stick Puzzles

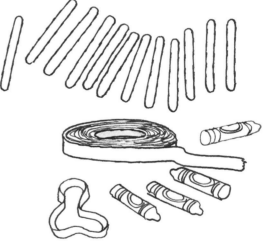

YOU NEED: 3 to 12 Popsicle sticks or tongue blades
tape
crayons or felt-tip markers
a rubber band

YOU DO:
1. Line up the Popsicle sticks evenly so that they are touching and straight like a picket fence.
2. Put two strips of tape across the sticks to hold them together, then number them from left to right.

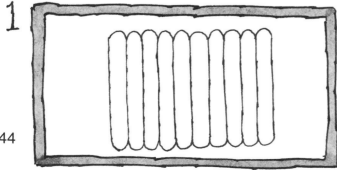

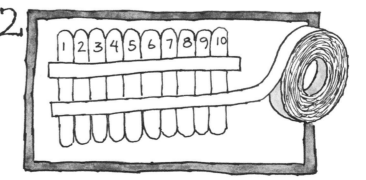

144

3. Turn over the sticks and draw a simple picture with crayons or markers, being sure that each stick has part of the design on it. Shapes, letters, and numbers are easy to work with.*

4. Then remove the tape, mix up the sticks, and put your puzzle back together. (Don't peek at the numbers unless you really need to.)

5. Put the rubber band around the sticks so you won't lose them. How about trading puzzles with each other?

*If you're younger, ask a grown-up to draw the picture for you so you can put the puzzle together with ease.

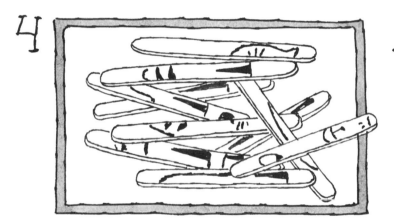

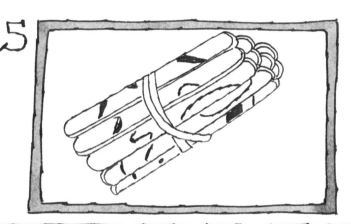

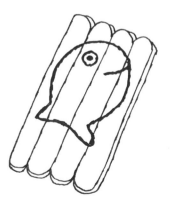

Another way: You can also glue a magazine picture onto the sticks; then cut the picture apart between the sticks when the glue is dry.

The best part of this activity is that you can make a puzzle that's *just right for you.* If you are a preschooler, draw a large picture on only 3 or 4 sticks. If you're older, you can use as many sticks as you'd like, and even draw pictures on both sides. (If you decide to do this, be sure to use different colors on each side so the pieces are not too difficult to match up.)

Magnet Maze

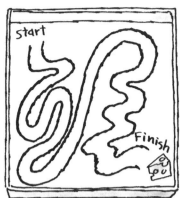

YOU NEED:
a box lid or piece of sturdy cardboard
crayons or felt-tip markers
construction paper
paper clips
tape or glue
a magnet

YOU DO:
1. Design a maze on the box lid, marking the Start and Finish.
2. Cut out a paper animal, such as a mouse, and tape a paper clip on the back.
3. Place the mouse on Start; then move the magnet *underneath* the cardboard to guide the mouse through the maze from beginning to end, trying not to touch the lines.
4. If you have a stopwatch, see how long it takes you. Then try to beat your record the next time.

Another way: Instead of a maze, you could draw a *baseball diamond* and move your "batters" all around the bases and back to home plate again. A home run is scored *only* if a player stays *on the lines* and touches every base. If he goes off a line or misses a base, he's out.

To make the game more challenging, set a time limit for running the bases.

Geo Board

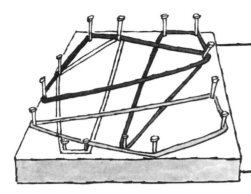

Hammer some nails into a scrap of wood. Now create designs by stretching rubber bands of different colors and sizes, or yarn or string, from one nail to another. Can you make a triangle? A rectangle? A hexagon? How about your initials? You might want to hang up your favorite design for a wall decoration.

Marble Tilt

YOU NEED:

a shallow box or box lid (a stationery or gift
  box with a see-through lid works well)
crayons or felt-tip markers
scissors
a marble

YOU DO:

1. Draw a few circles inside the box, making sure they are smaller than your marble.
2. Poke the scissors through the cardboard to cut out the circles.
3. Draw a design around each hole with your markers or crayons and number them for scoring points.
4. Drop in the marble and try to make it "land" in the holes by tilting the box. Can you picture your marble rolling into a bunch of daisies, lollipops on sticks, or the center of Rudolph's red nose?

Another way: Get someone to help you put together a *giant* marble game, using a large shallow box lid (like a dress box). With each player holding a corner, tilt the lid and see if you can get the marbles to land in the holes! If you want to keep score, assign a number to each hole. Just for fun, put a negative number or "no score" on one hole.

YESTERDAY'S NEWSPAPER

Don't throw away yesterday's newspaper or last month's magazines. They are never out of date for creative play at home or in the classroom. It's nice to keep some handy as a ready resource whenever you're looking for a quiet activity.

Comic Cut-ups

Let's start with the Sunday comics since they're large and colorful and can often be understood by the pictures alone.

1. Choose an easy one, like "Nancy," "Peanuts," or "Garfield."
2. Cut out each frame and glue it onto a separate piece of cardboard or construction paper.
3. Number the backs to help you check yourself later.
4. Shuffle the pictures, then try to put them back in the right order.

Other ways:

Hold back the *last* picture and take turns making up the ending. What do you think will happen next?

Choose just *one* of the comic frames and tell a story about it. What is everyone doing? Where are they? Can you tell how the characters feel by the looks on their faces?

148

Comic Sort-outs

1. Pick out four or five of your favorite strips.
2. Set aside a cardboard food tray for each comic strip you have chosen and glue a picture of the strip's *main* character on it.
3. Cut out lots of people and animals from your strips and put them into a pile.
4. Now match each character with the right tray. Did you get Linus and Charlie Brown together, Sluggo with Nancy, the dinosaur with B.C.?

Now that your comics are all sorted out, mix them up and play the game again!

Comic Mix-ups

Can you imagine Ziggy running away from a dinosaur, or Marmaduke and Garfield having a picnic together? Create new funnies by combining characters from many *different* comics.

1. First draw a row of squares or frames on construction paper or cardboard.
2. Cut out characters from a variety of comic strips. Glue them inside the frames, mixing them up to tell a story.
3. Color in the background and glue on cut-outs (a tree, house, telephone, chair, and so forth) to complete the scene.

Now enjoy telling each other the crazy, mixed-up stories you've created.

Comic Bubbles

Make up your own "talking" comic strip.

YOU DO:
1. Choose a favorite strip from Sunday's paper.
2. Glue white paper over the "talking bubbles" and write in new words.
3. You can also write your own "bubbles" with Comic Mix-ups.

Your own comic strips will make original greeting cards and party invitations.

Newspaper Hunts

SHOW ME (a game for two or more)

Use any newspaper or magazine that you have handy to play Show Me. One person looks for a picture and then asks the other to point to it when he finds it.

"Show me a squirrel."

"Show me a pocket on a coat."

Older children can look for even smaller details:

"Show me the number eight on a clock or on a sports uniform."

You can play Show Me wherever you are — on a bus, in a waiting room, or out on a walk. You'll always find a billboard, a sign, or something to "Show Me."

SHOPPING SPREE

If you're older, you can go on a Shopping Spree through the ads. Give each player the *same amount* of money to spend (for example, $35.00) and see who can stretch his dollars the farthest. How many groceries or school supplies could you buy with *your* pretend money?

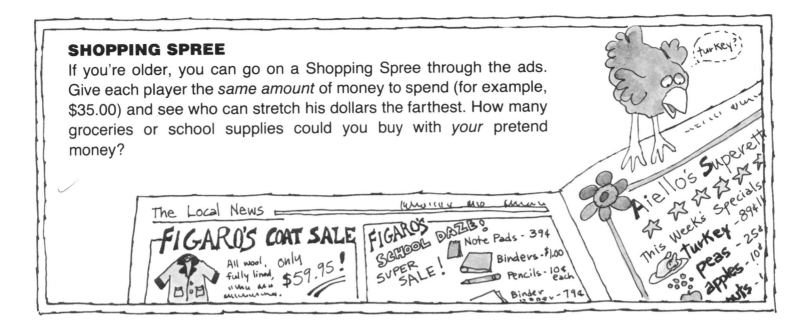

SPORTS QUIZ

Use your newspaper again for a Sports Quiz.

1. Look in the sports pages to see which teams are playing, and write down the names on cards or slips of paper.
2. Each player, in turn, draws a card from a bag until all the teams have been chosen.
3. Make up your own quiz and check the sports section to see who picked the lucky teams.

Sample quiz:

STORY TIME

BEDTIME

Five minutes, five minutes more, please!
   Let me stay five minutes more!
Can't I just finish the castle
   I'm building here on the floor?
Can't I just finish the story
   I'm reading here in my book?
Can't I just finish this bead-chain . . .
   It almost is finished, look!
Can't I just finish this game, please?
   When a game's once begun
It's a pity never to find out
   Whether you've lost or won.
Can't I just stay five minutes?
   Well, can't I just stay four?
Three minutes, then? Two minutes?
   Can't I stay one minute more?

by Eleanor Farjeon

It's hard to stop what you're doing when it's rest hour or bedtime, but sharing a storybook can make settling down easier. The activities that follow can be used for story time anywhere . . . in the classroom, in a waiting room, or at home. *Any* time is time to enjoy a story together.

Choosing a Story

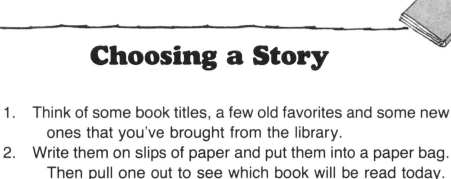

1. Think of some book titles, a few old favorites and some new ones that you've brought from the library.
2. Write them on slips of paper and put them into a paper bag. Then pull one out to see which book will be read today.

Another way: Fill a laundry bag with real books, or use your Yarn Thingamajig (p. 85) to help decide who chooses the story.

Match-up Game

Using the bag filled with book titles, name a character who goes with each book that you pick.

Another way: Make a card for each book and matching cards for the characters. Then you can use them to play matching games, like Label Concentration (p. 48) or Comic Sort-outs (p. 149), pairing up the characters with their books.

Josie Pig!

Storybook Pretending

With a little imagination, the classroom rug or your bed at home can become a magic place that changes with each story: the landing spot where Alice falls down, down, down; the corner of the barn where Charlotte spins her web; or Winnie the Pooh's hideaway in the forest. Close your eyes and *whoooshh!* You can imagine almost anything!

Book Buddies

Get to know your books even better by *pretending* you are one of the characters. With a hat and a few props you can feel like you are Robin Hood or even Paddington Bear.

Dress up your dolls and stuffed animals to get them into the act too. You could put overalls on any toy teddy bear and call him your Corduroy; any monkey could play the character Curious George. Something to cuddle in your arms will make the story seem almost real.

Another way to bring a book to life is to create a special storybook companion yourself. Following the basic directions for making an Autograph Hound (p. 119), sew and stuff an animal like one of the "*Millions of Cats*" or a ferocious "wild thing" with bulging eyes and sharp pointed teeth.

Make a stick puppet or a finger puppet (p. 100) to play the parts of your favorite storybook characters, or even sew a tiny "thimble puppet" to tuck into your pocket. Now all of these "book buddies" can be there to enjoy the stories right along with you.

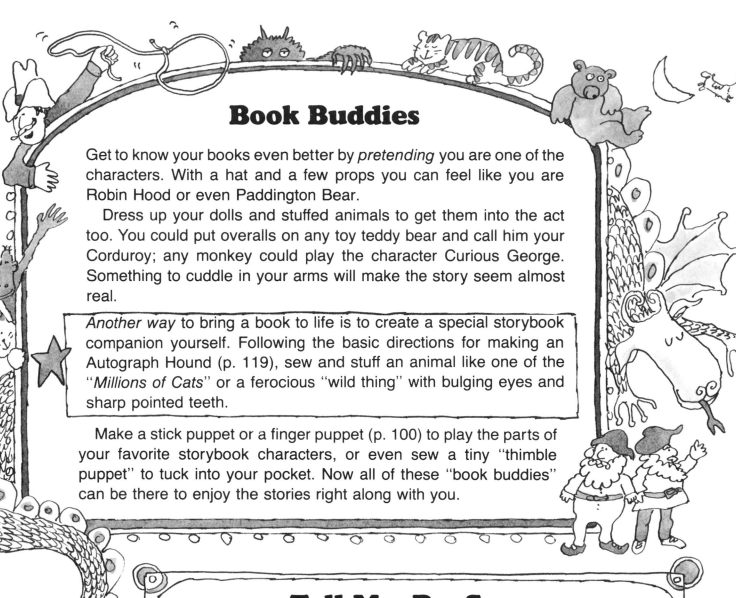

Tell Me, Dr. Seuss

Tape an interview with one of your favorite storybook characters or author.

INTERVIEWER: Tell me, Dr. Seuss, why do green eggs go with ham?

DR. SEUSS: Green eggs go with ham simply 'cause it rhymes with Sam.

Fan Mail

Write a letter to one of the characters telling why you wish you could change places with him . . . or why you wouldn't.

Dear Stuart Little,
What's it like to
live in a matchbox?
Don't you get all
cramped up?
Yours,
Carla

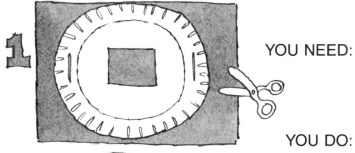

Dear Mr. Emberley,
I like to draw.
I like your books.
The Zortians
are my
favorite.
Love,
Benjamin

Mr. Ed Emberley
Little, Brown
Boston, Mass.

You could also write to the author of one of your favorite books to say what you especially liked about her book. (Writers really do like to hear from their readers, so address a letter to the author in care of the publisher.)

You can have fun with the *words* in your book too.

Window Words

YOU NEED: a paper plate
scissors
a long strip of paper
pencil or pen

YOU DO:
1. Cut a window in the center of the paper plate and a slit on each side large enough for the paper strip to slide through.
2. Write down words from the book you are reading on a slip of paper.

(continued next page)

155

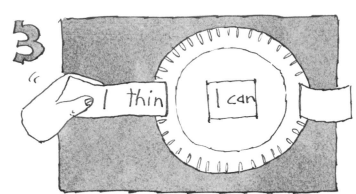

3. Put the strip through the slits and pull it across the back of the plate. As each word appears in the window, try to find it in your book. How often do you see "hush" in *Goodnight Moon?*

Other ways: Choose words or phrases that are special to a particular book (like "push-me pull-you," or "I think I can"). Can you guess the books where they can be found? (*Dr. Doolittle, The Little Engine That Could.*)

Make a word or picture dictionary to help you remember your new "window" words.

Book Themes

The next time you go to the library, choose a *theme* for the week and look for books that fit: colors, hats, nonsense, monsters, and so forth. Then plan a few storytime activities to go with each theme.

COLORS

You can do lots of crayon activities with these and other books about colors. See page 72 for some crayon ideas.

The Great Blueness — Lobel
Hailstones and Halibut Bones — O'Neill
Bear's Picture — Pinkwater
Harold and the Purple Crayon — Leisk
What Is a Color? — Provensen

HATS

Everybody loves books about hats! They're especially fun to read when you're wearing a hat you've made yourself. Trim a paper plate, pie pan, or berry basket with bits of ribbon or crepe paper and presto! you can be the characters in these well-known books about hats:

> *Caps for Sale* — Slobodkina
> *Cat in the Hat* — Geisel
> *Jennie's Hat* — Keats
> *The 500 Hats of Bartholomew Cubbins* — Geisel

NONSENSE

To get in the mood for nonsense books, play a silly game like Name Nonsense (p. 23) or I Adore My Pet Gorilla (p. 109).

> *Dr. Seuss* books — Geisel
> *Where the Sidewalk Ends* — Silverstein
> *The Man Who Sang the Sillies* — Ciardi
> *A Great Big Ugly Man Came Up and Tied His Horse to Me* — Tripp
> *Rain Makes Apple Sauce* — Scheer and Bileck

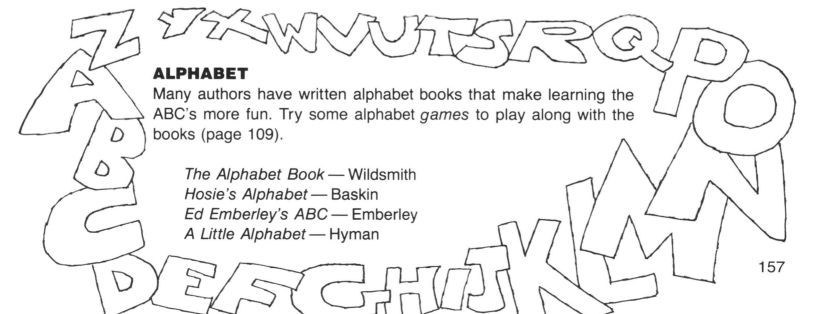

ALPHABET

Many authors have written alphabet books that make learning the ABC's more fun. Try some alphabet *games* to play along with the books (page 109).

> *The Alphabet Book* — Wildsmith
> *Hosie's Alphabet* — Baskin
> *Ed Emberley's ABC* — Emberley
> *A Little Alphabet* — Hyman

157

MEASURING

If you choose "measuring" for a theme, there are dozens of activities you can do using just a ruler, tape measure, or meter stick. See Moving Along (p. 116) and Garden Experiments (p. 61). Keep your measuring aids close by as you inch your way through these books.

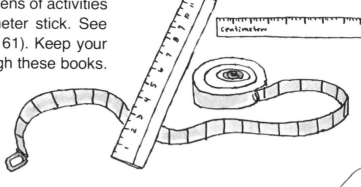

Inch by Inch — Lionni
Time and Measuring — Holl
Jim and the Beanstalk — Briggs
Metric Can Be Fun! — Leaf

MONSTERS

You won't be afraid of a monster once you make one yourself: a fiery dragon, a lazy lizard, a ghastly ghost. Create your pet monster out of junk materials, papier-mâché, or clay to keep you company and scare away all those wild things, zombies, and alligators.

Maybe a Monster — Alexander
Where the Wild Things Are — Sendak
There's a Nightmare in My Closet — Mayer
My Momma Says There Aren't Any Zombies, Ghosts or Vampires — Viorst
The Alligator Under the Bed — Nixon

A giant bookmark will hold the page where you got sleepy.

158

Bookmarks

HEADS AND TAILS

YOU NEED:

pencil and paper
thin cardboard, felt, or construction paper
felt-tip markers
scissors
yarn or ribbon
glue, tape, stapler, or brad fasteners

YOU DO:

1. Choose an animal, like a cat, mouse, or even a bookworm, and make a sketch of it.
2. Draw and cut out the head and body from cardboard, felt, or construction paper. Be sure that the body is as tall as most picture books so the head will peek out over the top.
3. Fringe a ribbon or braid some yarn for the tail.
4. Put your animal together with glue, tape, staples, or brad fasteners.
5. Add a stripe or spot to the body as you finish each book.

Another way: Make the animal's body by connecting circles, squares, or triangles, adding a shape whenever you read a new book. Watch your bookmark "grow" longer and longer!

Keeping Track

Keep track of the books you have read by building a train track on your wall or bulletin board. Each time you finish a book, write the title and author on a railroad tie. How many trips to the library will it take before the track stretches all the way across the room?

When storytime's over, it's often bedtime (or rest hour at school). Just a few minutes left to tuck away a "pillow surprise"—a little picture or a thoughtful note you've written to someone else.

Lights out!

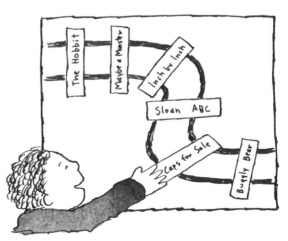

GUIDE TO LEARNING CONCEPTS FOUND IN
WINDING DOWN

This is the chapter that offers the most opportunities for imaginative play and self-expression. It encourages a child to make up stories, invent characters, play imaginary roles, and get acquainted with books.

ACTIVITIES (Page)	MOVEMENT/MOTOR COORDINATION large/small		CREATIVITY/MAKING THINGS	LANGUAGE DEVELOPMENT/COMMUNICATION oral/written	READING AND MATH SKILL-BUILDING	PROBLEM-SOLVING/DISCOVERY	IMAGINATIVE PLAY/SELF-EXPRESSION
Powwow (138)				X			X
Pass the Bug Box (138)		X	X	X	X		X
Add a Character (139)				X		X	X
Good Feelings (140)		X	X	X	X		X
Choose a Chore (140)	X			X	X		
Tape a Tale (141)				X			X
Cat Chat (141)				X			X
Sixty Seconds (142)				X		X	X
Do Your Own Radio Show (142)				X			X
Ad-libs (143)				X		X	X
Popsicle-Stick Puzzles (144)		X	X		X	X	
Magnet Maze (146)		X	X		X	X	
Geo Board (147)	X	X	X		X	X	
Marble Tilt (147)	X	X	X		X	X	
Comic Cut-ups (148)		X	X	X	X	X	X
Comic Sort-outs (149)		X			X	X	
Comic Mix-ups (149)		X	X	X	X		X
Comic Bubbles (150)		X	X	X	X		X
Show Me (150)		X		X	X	X	
Shopping Spree (151)				X	X	X	X
Sports Quiz (151)				X	X	X	
"Bedtime" (152)							
Choosing a Story (153)				X		X	
Match-up Game (153)		X			X	X	
Storybook Pretending (153)							X
Book Buddies (154)			X	X			X
Tell Me, Dr. Seuss (154)				X			X
Fan Mail (155)		X		X			X
Window Words (155)		X		X	X		X
Book Themes (156)							
Colors (156)		X	X				
Hats (157)		X	X				X
Nonsense (157)				X	X		
Alphabet (157)				X	X		
Measuring (158)		X			X		
Monsters (158)		X	X				X
Heads and Tails (159); Keeping Track (159)		X	X				

160

DATE DUE